ISO 9001:2000
for Small
and Medium
Sized Businesses

Also available from ASQ Quality Press:

ISO 9001:2000 Explained, Second Edition
Joesph J. Tsiakals, Charles A. Cianfrani, and John E. (Jack) West

ISO 9000:2000 Quick Reference
Jeanne Ketola and Kathy Roberts

ISO Lesson Guide 2000: Pocket Guide to Q9001:2000,
Second Edition
Dennis Arter and J. P. Russell

ANSI/ISO/ASQ Q9000:2000 Series Quality Standards

*Success through Quality: Support Guide for the Journey to
Continuous Improvement*
Timothy J. Clark

The Practical Guide to People-Friendly Documentation
Adrienne Escoe

The Certified Quality Manager Handbook, Second Edition
Duke Okes and Russell T. Westcott, editors

ISO 9001:2000
for Small
and Medium
Sized Businesses

Herbert C. Monnich, Jr.

ASQ Quality Press
Milwaukee, Wisconsin

ISO 9001:2000 for Small and Medium Sized Businesses
Herbert C. Monnich, Jr.

Library of Congress Cataloging-in-Publication Data

Monnich, Herbert C., 1932–
  ISO 9001-2000 for small and medium sized businesses / Herbert C. Monnich.
    p. cm.
  Includes bibliographical references and index.
  ISBN 0-87389-515-0 (alk. paper)
    1. ISO 9000 Series Standards. 2. Quality control—Standards. 3. Quality
  assurance—Standards. 4. Small business—Management. I. Title.

  TS156.6 .M66 2001
  658.5'62—dc21   2001031801

© 2001 by ASQ

10 9 8 7 6 5 4 3 2

ISBN 0-87389-515-0

Acquisitions Editor: Annemieke Koudstaal
Production Editor: Craig S. Powell
Production Administrator: Gretchen Trautman
Special Marketing Representative: Denise M. Cawley

ASQ Mission: The American Society for Quality advances individual and
organizational performance excellence worldwide by providing opportunities for
learning, quality improvement, and knowledge exchange.

Attention Bookstores, Wholesalers, Schools, and Corporations: ASQ Quality
Press books, videotapes, audiotapes, and software are available at quantity
discounts with bulk purchases for business, educational, or instructional use.
For information, please contact ASQ Quality Press at 800-248-1946, or write to
ASQ Quality Press, P.O. Box 3005, Milwaukee, WI 53201-3005.

To place orders or to request a free copy of the ASQ Quality Press Publications
Catalog, including ASQ membership information, call 800-248-1946. Visit our
Web site at www.asq.org or http://qualitypress.asq.org .

Printed in the United States of America

 Printed on acid-free paper

American Society for Quality

Quality Press
600 N. Plankinton Avenue
Milwaukee, Wisconsin 53203
Call toll free 800-248-1946
Fax 414-272-1734
www.asq.org
http://qualitypress.asq.org
http://standardsgroup.asq.org
E-mail: authors@asq.org

Table of Contents

Preface

The ISO 9000 family of quality standards was originally issued in 1987, and then was revised in 1994 to clarify some of the elements. However, even before the 1994 revisions were implemented, ISO Technical Committee (TC) 176 recognized that more sweeping changes were required. ISO Technical Committee 176, Subcommittee 2, Working Group 18 (ISO TC 176 SC 2 WG 18) was formed to update the standards and make them easier for all organizations to use. The ANSI/ISO/ASQ Q9000–2000 family of standards is the result of that effort. Some of the major changes are:

- A shift from documenting quality system procedures to focusing on developing and managing an organization's family of effective business processes. This is a major improvement, allowing small and medium sized businesses to establish and document a simple quality management system that meets the needs of his customer and his business while fully complying with ANSI/ISO/ASQ Q9001–2000 requirements.

- An approach built around a business process model rather than a manufacturing process model. This includes the use of wording that is easily understood in all sectors, not just the manufacturing sector.

- Greater emphasis on the role of top management. This is not much of a change for small and medium sized businesses, since top management has usually been deeply involved in the quality management system.

- More emphasis on the customer. Again, this is not as great a change for small and medium sized businesses since this is the way that most of them survive.

- Emphasis on the concept of continual improvement of the quality management system.

- Emphasis on setting measurable quality objectives.

- Emphasis on the analysis of data to define opportunities for improvement.

This book addresses the needs of small and medium sized organizations that:

- Want a general understanding of the concepts of ANSI/ISO/ASQ Q9001–2000, especially as they relate to small and medium sized businesses

- Want to develop a quality management system based on ANSI/ISO/ASQ Q9001–2000

- Want to update their ANSI/ISO/ASQC Q9001–1994-based quality management system to an ANSI/ISO/ASQ Q9001–2000-based system

This book explains the meaning and intent of the requirements of ANSI/ISO/ASQ Q9001–2000 and discusses how they relate to small and medium sized organizations involved in all product categories.

Chapter 1:

- Defines what small and medium sized businesses are

- Summarizes the insights obtained from organizations involved in the validation of the various drafts of the ANSI/ISO/ASQ Q9000–2000 family

- Summarizes the insights of small and medium sized businesses in the development and use of their registered quality management system

- Discusses the process approach concept used in the ANSI/ISO/ASQ Q9000–2000 family of standards

- Covers clauses 1, 2, and 3 of ANSI/ISO/ASQ Q9001–2000 including subclause 1.2 "Application" and acceptable and unacceptable exclusions

- Introduces some of the basic terminology from ANSI/ISO/ASQ Q9000–2000

- Explains the ANSI/ISO/ASQ Q9000–2000 family of standards, giving details on the "new" requirements

Chapters 2 through 6 discuss the requirements of clauses 4 through 8 of ANSI/ISO/ASQ Q9001–2000:

- Each subclause is discussed individually

- Every clause has a subheading called "Techniques for Small and Medium Businesses" which explains how the requirement can be implemented in smaller businesses

- Other subheadings identify the following guidance, indicating whether it is mandatory, useful, or just something you might want to consider:

  - Required and Suggested Documents

  - Required Documented Procedures

  - Optional Documented Procedures

  - Required Records

  - Recommended Records

Chapter 7 is an example of a quality manual with a sample procedure for a small business.

Chapter 1

ISO 9001 and Small and Medium Sized Businesses

THE ADVANTAGE OF BEING SMALL

This 2000 version of ISO 9001 makes it much easier for a smaller company to comply with the requirements. There are several reasons why this is true.

First, ISO 9001 is now much less prescriptive. The 1994 version of ISO 9001 required 18 documented procedures; the 2000 version only requires six documented procedures. Does this mean that your business only has to have six documented procedures? The answer is no! You have to have at least six procedures documented; what these procedures are is spelled out in the standard. These six procedures may be enough for your business. However, if they are not enough so that your business can operate effectively, then it is up to you to determine which and how many procedures you need for your business. The standard is now allowing you to determine what is necessary rather than prescribing what you have to do.

Chapter 7 of this text contains a sample quality manual for a small two-person company. The manual only refers to six separate documented procedures. This shows that it is possible to have a small system under ANSI/ISO/ASQ Q9001–2000. However, the experience of the employees and the simplicity of the operation also contribute greatly to the manual's ability to be short and succinct.

Second, two of the major changes or additions to ANSI/ISO/ ASQ Q9001–2000 are an increased emphasis on customer satisfaction and top management commitment and involvement. These are two areas where small and medium sized businesses generally excel. Usually, but not always, the management of smaller businesses is in close contact with their customers. This offers management an increased ability to evaluate and measure customer satisfaction. How this advantage can be used is detailed throughout this text. Also, the top management of smaller companies is usually involved in many of the day-to-day operations of the business. These managers know, understand, and take advantage of the benefits of an ISO 9001 system. They already are performing the tasks that are required of them by the new 2000 standard. This advantage is pointed out throughout this text also.

THE PROCESS APPROACH—WHAT IS IT?

The major change from the 1994 version of ISO 9001 to the 2000 version is the change in format. The old format was based on a manufacturing cycle, from order taking through design, purchasing, manufacturing, inspection, and shipping. It also covered management and support activities in its 20 elements. This system was easy to follow for a manufacturing organization but caused problems for most other types of organizations.

The 2000 version of ISO 9001 and 9004 follows a "process" approach. A process converts an input to an output using resources under controlled conditions. The process of frying an egg converts a raw egg (input) to a cooked egg (output), consuming resources (heat and your time) controlled by you. Combining a number of these processes can convert bread, milk, oranges, ground coffee beans, and a slab of bacon into a breakfast of bacon and eggs with orange juice and coffee.

Likewise, all organizations convert inputs into outputs through a number of processes. Each organization will use its own unique combination of processes to take human, monetary, material, and other resources as inputs and convert them into unique products and services. Organizations produce their product by identifying, linking, organizing, and managing these various processes.

Most businesses have several major, or "macro," groups of processes, including: general management, management of resources, product realization, and measurement and control. These are the basic process groups identified by the ANSI/ISO/ASQ Q9000–2000 series. The application of process approach is discussed later in this text under ISO subelement 4.1.

SMALL OR MEDIUM BUSINESSES

What do we mean when we say small or medium business? Small businesses have been categorized as businesses with less than 10 employees. Small businesses have also been categorized as businesses with less than 500 employees. Medium businesses have been defined as starting at 50 to 100 employees on the low end and going up to 250 to 500 employees on the high end. So actually, depending upon the purpose for the categorization, any reasonable answer is correct.

The size of a business influences the culture within the business. In small and medium businesses the chance for and the probability of effective communication between top management and the newest employee is quite good, the management structure is generally simple, and quite often the product or service provided by the business is simple rather than complex. For all these reasons, and for many similar reasons, it is easier for small and medium businesses to implement an effective ISO 9000 quality management system. These small and medium business quality management systems generally require less documentation than the quality management systems for large organizations.

Small businesses usually have an owner or manager plus one or two employees performing supervisory roles in key areas. Medium businesses have an owner or manager plus some managers of the larger functions performing such tasks as product or service delivery, finance, and marketing/sales.

ANSI/ISO/ASQ Q9000–2000 Validation Studies and Small and Medium Businesses

The size breakdown used by ISO TC 176 SC 2 WG 18 TG 1.8.2, who performed validations of committee drafts one and two (CD 1 and 2) and the Draft International Standard (DIS) of ISO 9001, was:

- Small businesses have less than 50 employees

- Medium businesses have from 50 to less than 250 employees

This size breakdown was effective and showed some differences between the groups, but not enough to separate small from medium businesses in the analysis of the validation studies.

Validation studies performed by TC 176 TG 1.8.2 used questionnaires from companies around the world to determine if:

- The 9001 and 9002 standards that were being developed met the needs of its customers and users

- It would be hard for the organizations to implement the revised standard

The studies showed that increased top management involvement and a greater emphasis on all forms of customer communication were areas that would take increased effort to implement. This was to be expected, since management involvement and customer satisfaction were, along with continual improvement, two of the most important areas that the drafters of the standard were seeking to emphasize.

Note: The validation studies included 240 replies from 23 countries. There were 97 service companies, 31 software manufacturers, 72 hardware manufacturers, and 104 material processors. (Some participants belonged to more than one category.)

The participants in the FDIS validation survey estimated that their time to implement was: less than three months—6 percent, 3 to 12 months—64 percent, more than 12 months—30 percent. (Data is from the 53 replies to the survey that answered this question.)

ISO 9000 Survey '99

The *ISO 9000 Survey '99* report,[*] prepared by Quality Systems Update and Plexus Corporation, gives insights to ISO 9000 implementation in small and medium sized companies in the United States and Canada. The study included data from 1150 respondents from 1055 companies representing a total of 3671 sites registered to ISO 9001/2/3:1994.

The study included 200 responses from companies with 49 or fewer employees, and 436 responses from companies with 50 to 249 employees. Table 1.1 shows some of the characteristics of these organizations.

The primary reasons for initiating ISO 9000 registration were: customer demand and expectation, internal quality benefits to the organization, and market advantage. Almost all of these participants felt that they had high quality demands from their customers along with a high degree of competition in their business area. About half also felt that they had high quality demands from regulators.

Table 1.1   Characteristics of small and medium businesses.

ISO 9000 Survey '99 **Report**

	Small	Medium
Number of Employees	26	121
1999 Annual Sales Volume	50 million	221 million
Standard Registered to: 9001 9002 9003	70 127 1	219 217 3
Manufacturing Services Software	114 76 7	336 86 11
Percent of participants that did not have a quality management system in place before ISO 9000	83	64

---

*Used with permission of the Quality Systems Update Publishing Company, 3975 University Drive, Suite 230, Fairfax, VA 22030; Tel: 703-359-8466; Fax: 703-359-8462; E-mail: isoeditor@aol.com.

After they had implemented ANSI/ISO/ASQC Q9001/2/3–1994, most of these organizations recognized the benefits of a quality management system. They felt that they were continuously improving, were sensitive to their customers needs, had established quality as a clear priority, and were seeking to eliminate problems at their source. In addition, ISO 9000 had led to the discovery of improvement opportunities in a majority of the organizations.

ISO has become the natural way of doing business for most of these companies. The documents, created in these companies for the purpose of registration, are used in daily practice and are regularly updated. In most of these companies, the design and development of the ISO 9000 system was customized to meet the needs of the business and included the integration of practices already in place.

ISO 9000 registrants also found the following business benefits:

- Improved customer satisfaction

- Improved productivity

- Improved sales performance

- Increased on-time delivery

- Increased outside sales contracts

- Improved cost of quality

- Increased market share

Registrants also found that they now had a new marketing tool, and some organizations reported observing improved export growth and experiencing an increase in employee retention.

The participants were asked what the most significant benefits were obtained as a result of achieving ISO 9000 registration. They reported that, externally, they had a higher perceived quality, a competitive advantage, and reduced customer quality audits.

Regarding the company's internal operations, the significant benefits the company experienced as a result of achieving ISO 9000 registration were: improved documentation, greater quality awareness by employees, and greater operational efficiency and productivity.

Table 1.2   Sources of ISO 9000 design and development.

ISO 9000 Survey '99 **Report**

Resource	Small	Medium
External consultant	97	125
Self-trained and self-developed internal leaders	76	165
Leaders trained and developed outside of the organization	52	142
External training provider	57	64
Leaders trained and developed inside of the organization	0	0

Almost all of the participants were aware of the revision planned for the ISO 9000 standards in 2000, and a majority of them were familiar with the proposed changes. The participants that were aware of the proposed changes supported them and were planning to continue with their registrations.

The participants were asked who had led the design and development of their ISO 9000 system. Table 1.2 shows the number of organizations that had significant input and leadership from the various resources.

ANSI/ISO/ASQ Q9000–2000 Family of Standards

The ANSI/ISO/ASQC Q9000–1994 family contained some 27 standards and documents. The ANSI/ISO/ASQ Q9000–2000 family consists of four primary standards supported by a considerably reduced number of other documents (guidance standards, brochures, technical reports, technical specifications). The four primary standards are:

1. ANSI/ISO/ASQ Q9000–2000: *Quality management systems—Fundamentals and Vocabulary*

2. ANSI/ISO/ASQ Q9001–2000: *Quality management systems—Requirements*

3. ANSI/ISO/ASQ Q9004–2000: *Quality management systems—Guidelines for Performance Improvements*

4. BSR/ISO/ASQ QE19011–2002: *Guidelines on Quality and Environmental Auditing*

The revised ISO 9001 and ISO 9004 standards were developed as a "consistent pair" of standards. The revised ISO 9001 addresses the quality management system requirements for an organization to demonstrate its capability to meet customer needs. The revised ISO 9004 goes beyond ISO 9001 toward the development of a comprehensive quality management system designed to address the needs of all interested parties, including the organization, employees, customers, suppliers, and society. ISO 9004 is an excellent reference for quality management system improvement ideas. Use it! Both standards use a common vocabulary as defined in ANSI/ISO/ASQ Q9000–2000 that also describes the underlying fundamentals.

The quality system audit standards ISO 10011 Parts 1, 2, and 3 are in the process of being revised jointly with environmental management system audit standards ISO 14010, 14011, and 14012. The combined standard, called ISO 19011: *Guidelines on Quality and Environmental Auditing*, is planned for publication in the third quarter of 2002.

The "Consistent Pair" of Quality Management Standards

The revised ISO 9001 and 9004 were designed to constitute a "consistent pair" of standards. Their structure and sequence are identical in order to make an easy and useful transition between them. They are "stand-alone" standards, but the parallel structure has resulted in an almost one-to-one agreement between the two. ANSI/ISO/ASQ Q9004–2000 *Quality management systems—Guidelines for Performance Improvements* has some additional elements, such as 4.3 "Use of quality management principles," 6.5 "Information," 6.6 "Suppliers and partnerships," 6.7 "Natural resources," and 6.8 "Financial resources," that are not in ANSI/ISO/ASQ Q9001–2000 *Quality management systems—Requirements*.

These ANSI/ISO/ASQ Q9000–2000 standards have global applicability. The consistent pair is applicable to all sizes of organizations and is less prescriptive. They are applicable to all product categories; they are now management process-oriented, not manufacturing-oriented. They are compatible with other management systems, such as ISO 14000 for environmental management.

They provide a consistent base and address the primary needs and interests of organizations in specific sectors, such as medical devices, automotive, telecommunications, aerospace, energy resource production (API), and others.

ANSI/ISO/ASQ Q9001–2000 CLAUSE 1 SCOPE

1.1 General

ANSI/ISO/ASQ Q9001–2000 specifies the *minimum* quality management system requirements for your organization when you:

- Need and *want* to demonstrate your ability to provide product that fulfills customer, regulatory, and your company's requirements.

- Intend to improve customer satisfaction through the effective application of your quality management system. This includes having processes for the *continual improvement* of the system and making sure that your products meet customer, regulatory, and your own company's requirements.

1.2 Application

The writers of the standard have worked to change the standard from a manufactured product-centered standard to a process-oriented standard. They have worked to remove the prescriptive documentation and recordkeeping requirements of earlier editions to create a standard that allows establishment of a system that meets the needs of your business. The requirements of the standard are applicable to all organizations regardless of your:

- Size

- Product

- Type of organization (for example, manufacturing, service, software, process)

The standard permits you to exclude requirements of the standard when you *cannot* apply it to your organization. These exclusions are all within clause 7 "Product realization." You must identify and justify these exclusions in your quality manual when you need to limit the application of the requirements. This reduced scope of your quality management system must also be clearly indicated in marketing materials and registration documents.

Unacceptable Exclusions

Requirements cannot be excluded where:

- You do not comply with the requirement of clause 4.2.2 a), which specifies providing justification for the exclusion of specific clause 7 "Product realization" requirements.

- Your organization decides not to apply a requirement of clause 7 based only on the justification that this was not a requirement of the 1994 ISO 9001, 9002, or 9003 editions and had not been previously included in your organization's quality management system.

- Requirements in clause 7 have been excluded because regulatory bodies do not require them, but they (the requirements) do affect your organization's ability to meet customer requirements. If you design and manufacture medical devices, but did not include design in your previous quality management system because the regulatory body did not require design, then you cannot continue to exclude design from your quality management system. If you choose not to include design, you cannot say that your system complies with ANSI/ISO/ASQ Q9001–2000.

- The overall responsibility for product realization belongs to your organization. The fact that a specific product realization process is subcontracted, purchased, or otherwise obtained outside of your organization does not permit the exclusion of this process from your quality management system. In fact, you must demonstrate that your organization has enough control over this process to assure that it conforms to your requirements, your customer's requirements, and the requirements of

ANSI/ISO/ASQ Q9001–2000. When you outsource processes, your quality manual must indicate that your quality management system covers the management of these processes.

Acceptable Exclusions

Exclusions may relate to product:

- If your organization has diverse products, you may choose to implement a quality management system for certain product lines as long as your quality manual, Quality Management System Certification, and any promotional material make it clear which products and services are covered by the quality management system. For example:

  - If you manufacture and service power equipment, pumps, bicycles, or similar products, you may want to establish a quality management system for the manufacturing of your product but not include the servicing.

  - If you manufacture precision gears and have a sideline business of carving decoys or welding up Bar-B-Q units, you may want to develop a quality management system for the gear manufacturing but not the sideline operations.

Exclusions are not meant to be only to entire clauses. There may be circumstances within your organization where specific requirements of one or more of the subclauses are applicable, while other subclauses can be excluded.

Subclauses of clause 7 that have been identified as possible areas of exclusion are:

- 7.3 "Design and development," where your organization does not have any responsibility for the design and development of your products. This occurs when you produce product designed by:

  - A customer, such as the machining of a casting or the construction of a building

  - A parent company, such as the canning of a proprietary soup

- 7.4 "Purchasing," if you mine, crush, and deliver crushed stone.

- 7.5.3 "Identification and traceability," where only the identification would be applicable to your products if traceability is not a requirement for your product. For example, if you manufacture high- and low-pressure fluid valves, you may have to maintain traceability for the components of the high-pressure valve but not the low-pressure valve.

- 7.5.4 "Customer property," where your organization does not use any customer property in your product or your product realization process. However, you must remember that soft products (for example, customer designs and proprietary processes and services, such as customer rail cars and trucks) are customer property.

- 7.5.6 "Control of monitoring and measuring devices," where your organization does not need measuring or monitoring equipment to furnish evidence of conformity of your product. This would be true if you are a banking institution, a legal office, a hotel, or an insurance firm.

QUALITY MANAGEMENT PRINCIPLES

An organization has a high chance for success if it implements and maintains a management system that is designed to continually improve performance at the same time that it addresses the needs of all interested parties. Eight quality management principles have been identified as a framework toward improving organizational performance. The principles form the basis for ANSI/ISO/ASQ Q9001–2000 and the other quality management system standards within the ISO 9000 family. ANSI/ISO/ASQ Q9000–2000 discusses these quality management principles in greater detail:

1. Customer focus—Organizations depend on their customers and therefore should understand current and future customer needs. They should meet customer requirements and strive to exceed customer expectations.

2. Leadership—Leaders establish unity of purpose and direction for the organization. Leaders should create and maintain an internal environment in which people can become fully involved in achieving the organization's objectives.

3. Involvement of people—People at all levels are the heart of an organization, and their full involvement enables their abilities to be used for the organization's benefit.

4. Process approach—A desired result is achieved more efficiently when activities and related resources are managed as processes.

5. System approach to management—Identifying, understanding, and managing interrelated processes as a system contributes to the organization's effectiveness and efficiency in achieving its objectives.

6. Continual improvement—Continual improvement of the organization's overall performance should be a permanent objective of the organization.

7. Factual approach to decision making—Effective decisions are based on the analysis of data and information.

8. Mutually beneficial supplier relationships—An organization and its suppliers are interdependent, and an equally beneficial relationship enhances the ability of both to create value.

ANSI/ISO/ASQ Q9001–2000 CLAUSE 2 NORMATIVE REFERENCE

ANSI/ISO/ASQ Q9001–2000 has only one official reference. That reference is ANSI/ISO/ASQ Q9000–2000 *Quality Management Systems—Fundamentals and vocabulary*. This document describes the fundamentals, including the eight quality management principles, upon which ANSI/ISO/ASQ Q9001–2000 is based.

The terms used in ANSI/ISO/ASQ Q9001–2000 to describe the supply chain are as follows:

supplier → *organization* → *customer*

The term "organization" replaces the previously used term "supplier." This means you, the unit to which the standard applies. The term "supplier" is now used instead of the previous term "subcontractor." The changes were made to reflect the popular usage of the terms.

ANSI/ISO/ASQ Q9001–2000 CLAUSE 3 TERMS AND DEFINITIONS

ANSI/ISO/ASQ Q9000–2000 also cites some of the unique terminology used in quality management systems. Some of the more important terms are listed in Table 1.3. You should refer to ANSI/ISO/ASQ Q9000–2000 for all of the terminology used and notes that will help you to better understand these terms and their application.

Earlier editions of ISO 9001 referenced ISO 8402. ISO 8402 has been replaced with Clause 3 of ANSI/ISO/ASQ Q9000–2000. ISO 8402 also included some dictionary terms such as "tender."

Table 1.3 ISO 9000 terms and definitions.

Term	Meaning	ANSI/ISO/ASQ Q9000–2000 Subclause Number
correction	action taken to eliminate a detected nonconformity	3.6.6
corrective action	action taken to eliminate the cause of a detected nonconformity or other undesirable situation	3.6.5
customer satisfaction	customer's perception of the degree to which the customer's requirements have been fulfilled	3.1.4
defect	nonfulfillment of a requirement related to an intended or specified use	3.6.3

Continued

Term	Meaning	ANSI/ISO/ASQ Q9000–2000 Subclause Number
document	information and its supporting medium	3.7.2
nonconformity	nonfulfillment of a requirement	3.6.2
preventive action	action taken to eliminate the cause of a potential nonconformity or other undesirable potential situation	3.6.4
procedure	specified way to carry out an activity or a process	3.4.5
process	set of interrelated or interacting activities which transforms inputs into outputs	3.4.1
product	result of a process	3.4.2
quality	degree to which a set of inherent characteristics fulfills requirements	3.1.1
quality assurance	part of quality management, focused on providing confidence that quality requirements will be fulfilled	3.2.11
quality control	part of quality management focused on fulfilling quality requirements	3.2.10
quality manual	document specifying the quality management system of an organization	3.7.4
quality objective	something sought, or aimed for, related to quality	3.2.5
quality plan	document specifying which procedures and associated resources shall be applied by whom and when to a specific project, product, process, or contract	3.7.5
quality planning	part of quality management focused on setting quality objectives and specifying necessary operational processes and related resources to fulfill the quality objectives	3.2.9
quality policy	overall intentions and direction of an organization related to quality as formally expressed by top management	3.2.4
record	document stating results achieved or providing evidence of activities performed	3.7.6
requirement	need or expectation that is stated, generally implied or obligatory	3.1.2
specification	document stating requirements	3.7.3
work environment	set of conditions under which work is performed	3.3.4

Source: ANSI/ISO/ASQ Q9000–2000

The developers of ANSI/ISO/ASQ Q9000–2000 intentionally excluded terms that were already defined in the Oxford English Dictionary. You will notice that the dictionary is the Oxford, or British English, dictionary; British English and French are the official languages of ISO documents.

YOUR QUALITY SYSTEM

You are about to develop your new quality management system. A word of caution: do not read a requirement into the standard that is not there. The requirements of ANSI/ISO/ASQ Q9001–2000 are good, basic requirements. Smaller companies can quite often address the requirements of the standard in simple but effective ways. Try to develop the most simple but effective way to address a requirement. Many times you will have a technique, or process, in place that addresses the needs of a requirement because you are running a successful business, and they are common sense processes that most businesses have had to implement in order to be successful.

A hierarchy of documents is generally used to describe a quality management system. The levels are generally described as:

- Tier 1: The quality manual (headed by the quality policy and objectives)

- Tier 2: Procedures

- Tier 3: Work instructions

- Tier 4: Forms

Small and medium businesses should combine these into two levels:

- Tier 1: The quality manual (headed by the quality policy and objectives, and including necessary procedures supported by effective forms)

- Tier 2: Work instructions and forms

NEW AND REFINED CHANGES TO ANSI/ISO/ASQ Q9001–2000

Some say that there are new requirements in ANSI/ISO/ASQ Q9001–2000, while others say that there are only clarifications of requirements that have always been there. I have seen quality management systems in some organizations that met the requirements of ANSI/ISO/ASQ Q9001–2000 even before work on the 2000 revision started, so perhaps the new revision *does* only contain clarifications.

However, for those that say that there are new requirements, TC 176 has identified "additional" requirements that were not in the earlier editions. Some of these requirements are in clauses of ANSI/ISO/ASQ Q9001–2000 that had no equivalent in ANSI/ISO/ASQC Q9001–1994. These requirements are summarized in Table 1.4. The other clauses that had corresponding clauses in ANSI/ISO/ASQC Q9001–1994 are summarized in Table 1.5.

In addition, many of the prescriptive requirements of ANSI/ISO/ASQC Q9001–1994 have been deleted. If you are implementing ANSI/ISO/ASQ Q9001–2000 from your system based on ANSI/ISO/ASQC Q9001–1994, you should review your quality management system, identify those procedures that you feel are not necessary for your organization, and discontinue their use. However, do not discontinue procedures that are no longer required just because it is permitted. If they are effective, continue their use. Tables 1.4 and 1.5 summarize information available through the standardsgroup.asq.org Web site. Visit the Web site for a more extensive description of the changes and improvements.

Table 1.4 New clauses in ANSI/ISO/ASQ Q9001–2000.

ANSI/ISO/ASQ Q9001–2000 Subclause	Description of New Requirement
1.2 "Application"	Describes the application of the standard and when requirements may be considered for exclusion.
5.2 "Customer focus"	Points out that top management is ultimately responsible for customer satisfaction including making sure that customer requirements are determined and met.

Continued

ANSI/ISO/ASQ Q9001–2000 Subclause	Description of New Requirement
5.5.3 "Internal communication"	Makes top management ultimately responsible for establishing appropriate communication processes and for making sure that communication occurs regarding the effectiveness of the quality management system.
7.2.1 "Determination of requirements related to the product"	Adds three new requirements to the process of determining customers' needs: b) Requirements not stated by the customer but necessary for specified or known intended use c) Statutory and regulatory requirements related to the product d) Any additional requirements determined by your organization
7.2.3 "Customer communication"	Requires your organization to determine and implement effective arrangements for communicating with customers concerning product: information; inquiries, contracts, or order handling, including amendments; and customer feedback, including customer complaints.
8.2.1 "Customer satisfaction"	Emphasizes that your organization must monitor information relating to your customer perception as to whether your organization has fulfilled your customer requirements.

Table 1.5   Improved and clarified clauses in ANSI/ISO/ASQ Q9001–2000.

ANSI/ISO/ASQ Q9001–2000 Clause	Description of New/Clarified Requirement	Corresponding ANSI/ISO/ASQC Q9001–1994 Clauses
1.1 "General"	The Scope has been refined to add the use of the effective application of the system, including processes for continual improvement to address customer satisfaction.	1 The requirements specified were aimed primarily at achieving customer satisfaction by preventing nonconformity.
3 "Terms and definitions"	Refers you to ANSI/ISO/ASQ Q9000–2000 *Quality management systems—Fundamentals and Vocabulary* and points out changes from the 1994 version: "organization" replaces "supplier," "supplier" replaces "subcontractor," and "product" includes "service."	3 Refer to ISO 8402 for definitions.

ANSI/ISO/ASQ Q9001–2000 Clause	Description of New/Clarified Requirement	Corresponding ANSI/ISO/ASQC Q9001–1994 Clauses
4.1 "General requirements"	There is more emphasis on the need for continuous improvement. The steps for implementing a quality management system are: a) Identify the processes needed for the quality management system b) Determine the sequence and interaction of these processes c) Determine criteria and methods needed to ensure that these processes are effective d) Ensure the availability of resources and information to operate and monitor these processes e) Monitor, measure, and analyze these processes f) Implement actions necessary to achieve planned results and continual improvement	4.2.1
4.2.1 "General"	The quality management system documentation must include: • Documents required by your organization to ensure the effective planning, operation, and control of your processes • Documented statements of a quality policy and quality objectives • A quality manual • Documented procedures and records required by the standard	4.2.2
4.2.2 "Quality manual"	Includes the requirement for your organization to specify and justify any exclusions in the quality manual. Your quality manual must also have a description of the interaction between the processes of your quality management system.	4.2.1
5.1 "Management commitment"	More emphasis is placed on top management commitment, especially communicating to your organization the importance of meeting customer, statutory, and regulatory requirements; establishing your quality policy; ensuring that your quality objectives are established; and ensuring the availability of resources.	4.1, 4.1.2.2, and 4.2.1

Continued

ANSI/ISO/ASQ Q9001–2000 Clause	Description of New/Clarified Requirement	Corresponding ANSI/ISO/ASQC Q9001–1994 Clauses
5.3 "Quality policy"	Top management must establish its policy for quality. Particular attention is given to subclause (b), which includes a commitment to comply with requirements and continually improve the effectiveness of the quality management system, and subclause (c), which provides a framework for establishing and reviewing quality objectives.	4.1.1
5.4.1 "Quality objectives"	The requirement for quality objectives, at relevant functions and levels within the organization, has been refined. The quality objectives must be measurable and consistent with the quality policy.	4.1.1 and 4.2.1
5.4.2 "Quality management system planning"	Managing change must be included in planning. Top management must make sure that the planning of the quality management system is carried out in order to meet the requirements given in *Quality management systems— General Requirements* subclause 4.1. Top management also must make sure that the quality objectives and the integrity of the quality management system are maintained when changes to the quality management system are planned and implemented.	4.2.3
5.5.2 "Management representative"	Top management must appoint a member of management to make sure that the awareness of customer requirements is spread throughout the organization.	4.1.2.3
5.6.2 "Review input"	The minimum elements that must be included in a management review are identified as: audit results; customer feedback; process performance and product conformity; the status of preventive and corrective actions; follow up of previous management reviews; changes that could affect the quality management system; and recommendations for improvement.	4.1.3

ANSI/ISO/ASQ Q9001–2000 Clause	Description of New/Clarified Requirement	Corresponding ANSI/ISO/ASQC Q9001–1994 Clauses
5.6.3 "Review output"	The key output requirements of a management review are identified as: improvement of the effectiveness of the quality management system and its processes; improvement of product related to customer requirements and resource needs.	4.1.3
6.1 "Provision of resources"	Emphasizes the requirement for an organization to determine and provide necessary resources to continually improve the quality management system effectiveness, and enhance customer satisfaction by meeting customer requirements.	4.1.2.2
6.2.2 "Competence, awareness and training"	The scope of this clause has been refined to include not only training needs but also competence and awareness.	4.18
6.3 "Infrastructure"	The organization must provide infrastructure needed to achieve conformity to product requirements including building, workspace, and associated utilities; process equipment; and supporting services.	4.9 Under this clause the primary requirement is to ensure that processes are carried out under controlled conditions.
6.4 "Work Environment"	The organization shall determine and manage the work environment needed to achieve conformity to product requirements.	4.9
7.1 "Planning of product realization"	The product realization processes must be under control. The term *process control* as referred to in ANSI/ISO/ASQC Q9001–1994 has been replaced with the term *product realization.*	4.2.3, 4.9, 4.10, 4.15, and 4.19
7.3.2 "Design and development inputs"	Clarifies the design input requirements that are to be met, including functional and performance requirements.	4.4.4
7.3.4 "Design and development review"	Clarifies that design and development reviews must be systematic in ensuring conformance with input requirements. In addition to recording reviews, the results of any necessary actions must be recorded.	4.4.6

Continued

ANSI/ISO/ASQ Q9001–2000 Clause	Description of New/Clarified Requirement	Corresponding ANSI/ISO/ASQC Q9001–1994 Clauses
7.3.7 "Control of design and development changes"	Includes a requirement for the organization to determine the effect of change on constituent parts and delivered product.	4.4.9
7.5.2 "Validation of processes for production and service provision"	Includes a requirement for the organization to carry out process validation.	4.9
8.1 "General"	Requires that monitoring, measurement, analysis, and improvement processes needed to demonstrate conformity of the product, ensure conformity of the quality management system, and continually improve the effectiveness of the quality management system must be planned and implemented, including the determination and use of applicable methods and statistical techniques.	4.10 and 4.20
8.2.2 "Internal audit"	States that selection of auditors and conduct of audits must ensure objectivity and impartiality of the audits. No restrictions on who the auditors may be.	4.17
8.2.3 "Monitoring and measurement of processes"	Has been refined by the requirement that the methods demonstrate the ability of the processes to achieve planned results.	4.20
8.4 "Analysis of data"	Focuses on the analysis of applicable data as one means of determining where continual improvement of the quality management system can be made, especially in the areas of: customer satisfaction; conformance to product requirements; characteristics and trends of processes and products (including opportunities for preventive actions); and suppliers.	4.14 and 4.20
8.5.1 "Continual improvement"	Requires that your organization must continually improve the effectiveness of the quality management system through the use of the quality policy, quality objectives, audit results, analysis of data, corrective and preventive actions, and management review.	4.1.3 and 4.9

Chapter 2

ANSI/ISO/ASQ Q9001–2000 Clause 4 Quality Management System

4.1 GENERAL REQUIREMENTS

Your organization must:

- Establish

- Document

- Implement

- Maintain

- Continually improve

a quality management system in accordance with the requirements of ISO 9001 if it wants to say that it is compliant with the standard.

Use of the process approach in the quality management system is addressed in the standard. Your organization must:

- Identify the processes needed

- Determine the sequence and interaction of these processes

- Determine criteria and methods to operate these processes

You then must:

- Ensure the availability of information to operate and monitor these processes

- Measure, monitor, and analyze these processes

- Implement actions necessary to provide planned results and continually improve these processes

The standard also points out that you are still responsible for the control of processes that you hire some other organization to perform.

 Techniques for Small and Medium Businesses

The best way to approach this requirement is to map the processes in your organization. You know what a road map is. It shows you how to get from one place to another and multiple routes that you can use. You can use a similar tool to identify and work with the processes in your organization. A technique used for mapping work processes is a simplified flowchart that uses only task blocks and decision diamonds. You can also use an outline technique for simple processes.

What are the processes in your organization? They start with the major process groups outlined in the standard, which are: organization management, resource management, product realization, and measurement and improvement.

These are groups of processes. What are the individual processes? In the product realization area they can consist of the following macroprocesses:

- Planning

- Customer-related processes

- Design and development

- Purchasing

- Production

- Control of monitoring and measurement devices

These are process levels that might be identified by upper management. However, as a purchasing agent, which processes might you be involved in? These processes might consist of:

- Supplier identification

- Supplier selection

- Purchasing procedures

- Supplier evaluation

- Verification of purchased product

Again, these processes can be broken down into smaller processes. As a receiving inspector, you might identify the following as your major processes:

- Purchase orders

- Receiving inspections

- Gage calibrations (notice this is a tie-in to one of the product realization processes)

- Nonconforming product control (another tie-in)

- Customer-owned property

From macroprocesses at the top, you can continue to break down into micro- and smaller processes at the more detailed end.

You need to address how your organization meets all of the requirements of ISO 9001. In many cases small or medium businesses do this just by conducting business on a day-to-day basis. Basically, you have to say what you do and do what you say. In some instances you will have to modify your normal operating systems slightly to address a requirement of the standard.

Your job is to establish the proper order or sequence of the steps you follow in running your business. You also need to determine how these processes tie in to each other. The process mapping or modified flowchart is an excellent tool to use to show the sequence of your processes and how they tie together. You should start with a primary level flowchart with only about 8 to 10 major processes. Then you can develop some secondary flow-charts to identify additional details of your system when necessary. For process mapping techniques, you may want to refer to *Mapping Work Processes* by Dianne Galloway, an excellent text available from ASQ Quality Press that simplifies the process mapping technique so that everyone in your organization can become involved.

Since you have to maintain and continually improve your quality management system, it helps to have a quality management system that is realistically documented. A basic system can be modified quickly and easily.

While you are developing and documenting your quality management system, consider implementing the changes outlined for your daily operations, especially if the modifications are minor. This enables you to spread the implementation over a period of time and will cause less disruption of the day-to-day operations of your business. This technique is hard to use in a large organization because of the long length of the communication chain.

In summary, you should:

- Identify the major process groups

- Draw process maps showing their interrelationships

- Implement changes as you develop your system, especially the easy but important changes

- Keep your system and documentation up-to-date

When you choose to purchase any management processes (for example, design or product realization processes, such as heat treating or measuring device calibration), you still must maintain control over these processes, and state that you are doing so in your quality manual. You must do this for all processes that you outsource whenever the process might affect your product's ability to meet requirements.

4.2 DOCUMENTATION REQUIREMENTS

4.2.1 General

Your quality management system documentation has to include the documents required by your organization to make sure that you have effective planning, operation, and control of your processes. This includes the six documented procedures that are required by the standard. You must also have documented statements of a quality policy and quality objectives, a quality manual, and the records required by the standard. The extent of your quality management system documentation will be dependent on the size and type of your organization, the complexity and interaction of your processes, and the competence of your personnel.

One of the most important considerations of this element is: What are the documents and documented procedures that you need to effectively operate your business? Here the key word is *effective*. The standard only requires the procedures stipulated in six clauses:

1. Clause 4.2.1 "Document control"

2. Clause 4.2.4 "Control of records"

3. Clause 8.2.2 "Internal quality audits"

4. Clause 8.3 "Control of nonconformity"

5. Clause 8.5.2 "Corrective action"

6. Clause 8.5.3 "Preventive action"

However, can your organization effectively operate your business with only these six documented procedures? The fictitious company whose manual is described in chapter 7 does. However, the manual is for a two person company that has been making a simple product for years, with partners that have highly developed management and artisan skills.

Techniques for Small and Medium Businesses

When do you need a documented procedure? When the procedure is complex or the persons performing the task could fail to do it correctly without the documented procedure. One test is to examine the output of several people performing the same task. If the outputs are identical, you may not have to document the procedure.

On the other hand, you may want to document the procedure for training purposes or for historical reasons. Only your organization can determine which procedures it feels need documentation. Of course, the final test is: Is your quality management system as effective as it could be without a documented procedure as it would be with the procedure documented?

Since you are only a small to medium organization, the extent of your quality management system documentation will probably be relatively short—especially if your product is uncomplicated and your management system is straightforward. Systems for manufacturers of more complex products, such as made-to-order computer hardware, would probably require greater detail in parts of the system documentation. Another major factor is the competence of your personnel. If you have a fast food restaurant with high personnel turnover, your need for detailed documentation will be greater than if you have a gourmet restaurant with professional chefs.

You may want to consider documenting:

• Complicated procedures

• Procedures that must be followed in exact sequence

• Procedures that have to be followed by a diverse group of people

Table 2.1   Documentation terminology.

Term	Definition
Document	Information and its supporting medium
Guideline	Document stating recommendations or suggestions
Procedure	Specified way to carry out an activity or a process
Quality Manual	Document specifying the quality management system of an organization
Quality Plan	Document specifying which procedures and associated resources shall be applied by whom and when to a specific project, product, process or contract
Record	Document stating results achieved or providing evidence of activities performed
Specification	Document stating requirements

Source: ANSI/ISO/ASQ Q9000–2000

We will cover the subject of quality policy and quality objectives under clause 5. We will discuss the quality manual and the control of documents and records later in this section.

ANSI/ISO/ASQC Q9001–1994 required 18 documented procedures; ANSI/ISO/ASQ Q9001–2000 requires only six. The details of these six documented procedures will be covered under the appropriate clauses. The standard also requires that you have documents that will ensure the effective planning, operation, and control of your processes. But what are documents? Documents take several different forms, according to ANSI/ISO/ASQ Q9000–2000. Table 2.1 shows what these types of documents are.

The standard only requires three specific documents. These documents are:

- Quality policy (clause 4.2.1.a)

- Quality objectives (clause 4.2.1.a)

- Quality manual (clause 4.2.1.b)

There are many areas where you might find documents helpful in the operation of your organization. These are the documents referenced by clause 4.2.1.d, which also may help you demonstrate compliance to the requirements of ANSI/ISO/ASQ Q9001–2000. Examples of documents that you may want to use include:

- Clause 4—process maps

- Clause 5—quality plans, process maps

- Clause 6—organization charts, internal communications such as memos and e-mails

- Clause 7—production schedules; production routings; industry, national, and international standards; approved supplier lists

- Clause 8—audit schedules

The standard is specific on what records must be included in your quality system, unless you have excluded the subelement (see Table 2.2). You also need to determine what other records you want to maintain.

4.2.2 Quality Manual

The standard requires that you establish a quality manual. This manual does not have to be a stand-alone document. If other parts of your operations are documented, the quality manual may be included in this documentation. The standard also stipulates that the minimum content of the manual is:

- The scope of the quality management system, that is, the range of the activities and products of your organization that are covered by your quality management system.

- The details of and justification for any exclusions. If your organization chooses to exclude any of the concepts of clause 7 of ANSI/ISO/ASQ Q9001–2000, you must explain why they are not applicable to your organization. In addition, these exclusions must have no effect on your product or service as previously discussed under ANSI/ISO/ASQ Q9001–2000 clause 1.2.

- The documented procedures required by the standard plus the procedures that your organization feels it requires. If you do not want to have the procedures themselves in your quality manual, then you must make reference to them.

Table 2.2 Records required by ANSI/ISO/ASQ Q9001–2000.

Clause	Record Required
5.6.1	Management reviews
6.2.2 (e)	Education, training, skills, and experience
7.1 (d)	Evidence that the realization processes and resulting product fulfill meet requirements
7.2.2	Results of the review of requirements relating to the product and actions arising from the review
7.3.2	Design and development inputs relating to product requirements
7.3.4	Results of design and development reviews and any necessary actions
7.3.5	Results of design and development verification and any necessary actions
7.3.6	Results of design and development validation and any necessary actions
7.3.7	Results of the review of design and development changes and any necessary actions
7.4.1	Results of supplier evaluations and necessary actions arising from the evaluations
7.5.2 (d)	As required by the organization to demonstrate the validation of processes for product and service provision where the resulting output cannot be verified by subsequent monitoring or measurement
7.5.3	The unique identification of the product, where traceability is a requirement
7.5.4	Customer property that is lost, damaged, or otherwise found to be unsuitable for use
7.6 (a)	Standards used for calibration or verification of measuring equipment where no international or national measurement standards exist
7.6	Validity of previous measuring results when measuring equipment is found not to conform with its requirements
7.6	Results of calibration and verification of measuring equipment
8.2.2	Internal audit results
8.2.4	Evidence of product conformity with the acceptance criteria and indication of the authority responsible for the release of the product
8.3	Nature of the product nonconformities and any subsequent actions taken, including concessions obtained
8.5.2 (e)	Results of corrective action
8.5.3 (e)	Results of preventive action

Source: ISO/TC 176/SC 2/N525R

- A description of the interactions between the processes of your quality management system. This is basically a description of how you do business and how you meet the requirements of the standard. You can use process maps or write down how your management system meets each of the requirements or why certain elements or subelements of clause 7 do not apply. This is not a short task, but it is relatively simple when you approach it one requirement at a time.

Required and Suggested Documents

The quality manual must be controlled and therefore must be documented.

Optional Documented Procedures

You may want to develop and follow a procedure for the control of the quality manual.

 Techniques for Small and Medium Businesses

Most of the time it is better for small and medium organizations to include procedures in the quality manual because of the limited documentation required of smaller organizations due to their general, basic simplicity. The limited documentation is also the result of the more realistic documentation requirements of ANSI/ISO/ASQ Q9001–2000.

4.2.3 Control of Documents

Documented procedures for your quality manual should be simple—no more than a couple of pages. Remember that these are tools for the trained individual to use and only cover the main steps of the procedure. They are not meant to be the instruction manual for a new employee. The longest procedures should never take up more than five to six pages.

If you remember your old English courses, you probably remember the five Ws and the H: who, what, when, where, why, and how. Procedures usually indicate who, what, when, where, and how. Why may or may not be included in procedures. Why, of course, explains the reason for performing the task or following a procedure. In some cases, the reason may be somewhat obvious. In other situations, including the why will help the acceptance and use of the procedure. A procedure may contain the major sequence of steps but leave the details to work instructions. In some cases, the detailed steps can be included in the procedure itself. For example, a manufacturing organization may have a general procedure for handling work orders and use work instruction documents like routings, prints, and specification sheets to give the detailed manufacturing instructions. The same organization may have the procedure for performing a management review in a single document.

In some cases it is not necessary to have procedures or instructions. A wholesaler may have a sales form with blank spaces to be filled out. A coding technique, such as an asterisk or bold type, is used to show where certain fields must be completed. A similar electronic technique would use required and optional fields.

What makes a controlled document? A controlled document will have:

- A unique identifier, such as a document number

- A page number (for example, page 1 of 4, page 1-4)

- Date issued (for example, June 27, 2000, 6/27/2000, 6/27/00, 27/6/2000)

- Approval (the name or initials of the approving authority, sometimes accompanied by position title, either a handwritten signature or an electronic signature)

- Document content (the actual content of the document)

A controlled document may also have:

- An organization name, such as ABC Company

- A title, such as Procedure Development

- A revision indicator (for example, Rev. A, -001, or just a blank if it is the original document)

- *Prepared by* or *Issued by* (name sometimes accompanied by a department and/or title)

The standard requires you to have a documented procedure explaining how you control your documents. Records are documents; however, they have some unique requirements that we will discuss later. Your documented procedure must have controls to make sure that:

- Documents are approved before being issued

- Documents are reviewed and updated as necessary, and that they are reapproved before being issued

- Changes in the document are identified

- Current revision status is documented

- Relevant versions of applicable documents are available where needed for use

- Documents remain legible

- Documents are easily identified

- Documents received from other organizations are identified and have controlled distribution

- Obsolete documents are not accidentally used

- Obsolete documents, if kept for any reason, are suitably identified

Your documents and documented procedures may be in any form or type of medium—paper or electronic. Procedures can be mounted on walls in factories, kitchens, offices, and other places of business. Consider where you have seen procedures for operating equipment, cooking food, and other tasks mounted on the walls of businesses.

Required Documented Procedures

The standard requires that your quality management system documentation must include a procedure for the control of documents.

 Techniques for Small and Medium Businesses

- Draw a flow diagram of your major processes

- Determine what procedures already exist in your organization

- Create a list of procedures you need to develop

- Identify where you need the procedures to be documented

- Develop, approve, and implement your document control system

---

4.2.4 Control of Records

You need to set up and maintain records for at least two reasons: (1) to provide the evidence that your products conform to requirements, and (2) to provide evidence that the operation of your quality management system is effective. As with other quality documents, records must:

- Remain legible

- Be easily identified

- Be retrievable

You need to write a documented procedure that defines the following controls for your records:

- Identification

- Storage

- Protection

- Retrieval

- Retention times

- Disposition

The identification of records usually follows the customs of your business. Storage can continue to be the technique that you have used in the past. Also, you can generally continue to use the same protection and retrieval systems that you have been using.

Retention times and disposition are the control mechanisms that create the most problems. Many organizations do not establish retention times nor dispose of records at the end of fixed retention times. Perhaps the most critical aspect of retention times is the minimum time that the record will be maintained. However, some organizations have encountered problems when they have kept documents too long.

The following is an example of a procedure for controlling records. See chapter 7, "A Sample Quality Manual," for an example of the procedures used in a small company.

ABC COMPANY PROCEDURE 2
CONTROL OF RECORDS

1.1 Records are handled following the procedures described in the applicable sections of the quality manual. These procedures document how the records demonstrate the achievement of the required quality. Pertinent supplier records, as explained in the procedures, are considered records to be maintained by ABC Company.

The following list addresses the document management aspects of various ABC Company records:

- Management reviews

- Education, training, skills, and experience

Continued

- Evidence that the realization processes and resulting product fulfill requirements

- Results of the review of requirements relating to the product and any necessary actions

- Design and development inputs

- Results of design and development reviews and any necessary actions

- Results of design and development verification and any necessary actions

- Results of design and development validation and any necessary actions

- Results of the review of design and development changes and any necessary actions

- Results of supplier evaluations and any necessary actions

- Records required by the organization to demonstrate the validation of processes, where the resulting output cannot be verified by subsequent monitoring or measurement

- The unique identification of the product, where traceability is a requirement

- Customer property that is lost, damaged, or otherwise found to be unsuitable for use

- Standards used for calibration or verification of measuring equipment where no international or national measurement standards exist

- Validity of previous results when measuring equipment is found not to conform to its requirements

- Results of calibration and verification of measuring equipment

Continued

- Internal audit results

- Evidence of product conformity with the acceptance criteria, and indication of the authority responsible for the release of the product

- Nature of the product nonconformities and any subsequent actions taken, including concessions obtained

- Results of corrective action

- Results of preventive action

Document and record management elements are listed in the following table. The primary record management characteristics are documented for ABC Company documents and records in subsequent tables.

Document and Record Management Elements.

Element	Content
Content	What information or record is in the record or file? If it is a compilation of subrecords, list the titles of the subrecords.
Identification	Title and unique identifier. Title should be meaningful and reflect purpose of the record. Numeric and alphanumeric codes can be used. Identifiers can include revision number and date.
Collection	List of locations where the records are collected and kept. Retention times must be the same for all copies.
Indexing	Identifies the information in the record and possibly the location. A record may have more than one identifier.
Access	How access is attained and who is allowed.
Filing	Filing format (paper, electronic, microfilm). Filing equipment and location.
Storage (including retention periods)	Storage facilities.
Maintenance	How records are maintained in useable condition for the retention time.
Disposition	Record disposal.

Continued

1.2 ABC Company prevents degradation of records by storing them in normal record filing or storage equipment facilities (for example, file cabinets, file storage boxes, electronic archives). The adequacy of the environment is determined by the records' usable condition at the end of the minimum storage period.

1.3 Records shall be considered retrievable if they can be obtained in a reasonable period of time. Recent records are generally retrievable within hours. Older records may take longer to retrieve (days), especially if they have been archived off site.

1.4 Records entirely generated by computer may have approvals generated by computer in lieu of signature. Handwritten signatures (or initials) and date shall be required on other records when specified.

Required Documented Procedures

The standard requires that your quality management system documentation must include a procedure for the control of records.

Techniques for Small and Medium Businesses

- Identify the various records your organization maintains

- Determine if these records are adequate or need to be improved

- Review Table 2.2 for required records

- Determine what new records are necessary

- Develop your record control system

- Implement your control system for all of your records

Chapter 3

ANSI/ISO/ASQ Q9001–2000 Clause 5 Management Responsibility

5.1 MANAGEMENT COMMITMENT

Top management must show proof of its commitment to the development, implementation, and continual improvement of your quality management system. This shows increased emphasis on management involvement and commitment from the earlier versions of ISO 9001. Right at the beginning of the management responsibility clause of the standard, top management is told what its primary responsibilities to the quality management system are:

- Establishing the quality policy of your organization

- Establishing measurable quality objectives that tie in to your quality policy

- Participating in management reviews

- Upholding the quality program and system (by communicating its importance, especially the importance of meeting customer requirements as well as statutory, legal, and regulatory requirements)

Techniques for Small and Medium Businesses

Experience has shown that the success of a quality management system is dependent upon top management commitment and involvement. Smaller companies have an advantage over larger companies because the top managers see and work with most of their employees on a regular basis. All that top management has to do is to show commitment both in words and deeds. There are three basic steps:

- Explain this commitment in regular meetings and ISO 9000 training meetings

- Back up this commitment in day-to-day activities, decisions, and communications

- Absolutely do not counteract this commitment by negative actions, which are one of the major causes for lack of success in the implementation and maintenance of many quality programs

Top management also shows its commitment to the quality management system by conducting management reviews and ensuring the availability of necessary resources.

Quality policies are discussed under clause 5.3 "Quality policy;" quality objectives are discussed under clause 5.4 "Planning;" management reviews are discussed in clause 5.6 "Management review;" resources are discussed under clause 6 "Resource management."

5.2 CUSTOMER FOCUS

Top management is also given the responsibility for making sure that your organization is focused on the customer. Top management is ultimately responsible for customer satisfaction. They do this through their own actions and by establishing a program that makes sure that your organization determines what the customer requirements are.

The standard does not go into detail on how your organization is to determine customer requirements in this element. However, subelement 7.2.1 "Determination of requirements related to the product" in element 7.2 "Customer-related processes" expands on this requirement. Subelement 7.2.1 points out that part of the responsibility of your organization is to determine the specific requirements stated by the customer. The other part of your organization's responsibility is to determine the requirements necessary for the product's intended use, plus statutory and regulatory requirements related to the product.

Since these additional "intended use," statutory, and regulatory requirements must be determined, it is up to management to make sure that your quality management system addresses these issues. Often this requires additional effort beyond just writing down the information off of a customer's purchase order or from a customer phone order.

Techniques for Small and Medium Businesses

In large organizations, it may be necessary to establish somewhat complex documentation and reporting structures to make sure that customer comments reach intermediate and top management reliably, consistently, and in a reasonable time frame. However, top management of most small and medium companies has the advantage of being very close to, and therefore can work directly with, the customer.

Top management of smaller businesses often receives input directly from customers. The product

Continued

requirements are handled through the sales or contract process. Regulatory and legal requirements relative to their business are usually known and handled in a routine manner. Customer concerns are handled directly by management.

You need to address customer satisfaction since your ISO 9001 system requires that you be customer-centered. However, how do you measure customer satisfaction? You can evaluate customer satisfaction by measuring:

- The number of customer complaints
- The severity of customer complaints
- Your customers' opinion of your organization, from a formal rating system based on questionnaires sent to customers, or any quantitative or qualitative system you may develop
- Feedback from customers, both positive and negative
- Your ability to obtain new customers
- Your ability to retain old customers
- Other metrics of customer satisfaction that provide you with the information you need

You do not have to use all of these measurements of customer satisfaction, but you should include some of them.

You may want to use a customer contact log or journal if you feel that this would assist you in following trends of customer comments. Your

Continued

> organization may want to consider using customer-contact report forms if there are many functions that come into contact with the customer.
>
> Your top management must decide what techniques will be used to show commitment to customers and customer satisfaction. Whatever techniques your organization uses, describe them briefly in your quality manual.

5.3 QUALITY POLICY

Your quality policy is the center point of your quality system and should describe the philosophical goals that your organization expects to achieve. Your organization needs to discuss what they want your quality policy to be. The quality policy goals that are set for your organization must be measurable, otherwise you cannot see if you are reaching them.

The quality policy for your organization must be appropriate to why your organization exists. It is the basis, or footing, of your quality management system. Everything, including your quality objectives, builds upon it.

Everyone in your organization should understand what your quality policy is and what it means. If they do not understand your organization's quality philosophy, then they will not know how to fit into your organization's quality culture.

Your organization must regularly review its quality policy as the organization changes and matures. It is a living document and must change as you change.

Required and Suggested Documents

The quality policy must be documented and is usually a separate document or one of the first documents at the beginning of the quality manual.

Techniques for Small and Medium Businesses

Have your top management discuss what the quality policy of the organization really is. At first glance this may seem easy, but it really requires thought. Management can involve whatever functions they choose in these discussions. Be sure to document the policy.

Some of the questions that they may want to ask themselves as they relate to quality are:

- What needs are being met by our organization?

- What goods and services do we and will we provide?

- Who are our stakeholders (customers, employees, shareholders, community)?

- What beliefs and values form our culture?

- Where are we headed philosophically, operationally, and competitively?

To spread the quality philosophy, discuss your quality policy in meetings involving all of your people so that there can be a flow of ideas. Hold several smaller meetings if one large meeting is not possible. Try to have a cross section of your employees in your meetings. One of the best tools that help you determine if you are complying with your commitment to continual improvement is to measure the success of your preventive and corrective action programs.

5.4 PLANNING

5.4.1 Quality Objectives and 5.4.2 Quality Management System Planning

The various functions in your organization, unless you are an extremely small organization, need to establish functional objectives that enable the company's quality objectives to be met. The individual functions include sales, production, design, and others that affect the quality performance of your organization. These functional quality objectives must also be measurable.

Quality planning also includes ensuring that adequate resources are available to allow your organization to achieve your quality objectives. Resources are discussed under clause 6.1 "Provision of resources."

Your quality planning needs to address all of your quality management system processes, including the reasons why you might be excluding some of the processes of section 7 of ANSI/ISO/ASQ Q9001–2000. The reasons for permissible exclusions were discussed earlier under clause 1.2 "Application."

When you make changes in your quality system, you need to make sure that:

- The changes are known by all affected functions

- Necessary documentation has been distributed

- The changes are implemented and watched to ensure that they do not cause disruptions

The processes of the quality management system may be documented in the quality manual, in flowcharts, or in separate procedures.

Required and Suggested Documents

Quality objectives have to be documented since you must measure how well your organization meets them.

Optional Documented Procedures

You may want to document a procedure describing how you develop your quality objectives, how your quality planning takes place, and how you update your quality objectives and plans.

 Techniques for Small and Medium Businesses

The first step in establishing your quality objectives is to determine your primary measurements. Remember that they must be quantifiable and should be indicators of success or failure.

Primary measurements for quality objectives must be based on your quality policy. Include, at a minimum, the function managers of your organization in the planning of your quality program measurements. This is especially true if they were not involved in the establishment of the quality policy.

Keep these measurements to a minimum. There are no guidelines for the number of measurements, but if you select too many you will probably be selecting subsets of a prime measurement. These measurements should be representative of a wide range of the organization's interests in order to get buy-in from all functions involved.

These measurements must be clearly defined. What are the inputs, the sources of data? How is the data to be analyzed? What are the units of measurement? Are there weighing factors or will they be pure numbers or percentages? What will the outputs be? How frequently will the results be reported? Will the data be just for the last period? Will moving averages or similar blending of measurements be used? How

Continued

will the data be reported? Will charts or graphs be used? Will the data be analyzed for trends?

Next you should tie your objectives to one of the primary measurements. For instance, If you are a service industry, one of your objectives might relate to customer service responsiveness with waiting time, satisfactory completion of service, and friendliness of your service representatives included in the basic objective and measurement.

Increased effectiveness of manufacturing might be a manufacturing objective. Reduction of scrap and rework, improved first piece inspection setup acceptance, and reduced cycle times might be some elements that you would want to include. Sales order and invoice accuracy may be elements in almost all businesses. On-time delivery would apply to both manufacturing and some service industries.

Make sure that all objectives are compatible throughout the organization. Increased production of a non-bottleneck operation might help a manufacturing function improve its efficiency, but would not necessarily improve the effectiveness of the organization if it caused an increase in inventory investment and expense.

The objectives for a function or process must be developed by the process owners to promote buy-in. Process owners are also better able to establish logical, specific, and attainable targets for the objectives.

Remember that you will be analyzing this data during management reviews. You should also analyze it as often as it would provide you meaningful information to operate your business.

5.5 RESPONSIBILITY, AUTHORITY, AND COMMUNICATION

5.5.1 Responsibility and Authority

The authority and responsibilities of all of the functions must be known. Confusion can result when individuals and functions do not know their own responsibilities and authorities, or those of others in the organization. In some cases, two people will try to perform the same function, causing duplication of effort or, worse yet, divergent results. In other situations, some task may be left unperformed because each person thought that the other person was going to do it.

Responsibilities and authorities can be established by job or function descriptions when documentation is necessary, or the same results can be attained informally as long as the organization maintains consistency and everyone knows their responsibilities and authorities. Individuals may wear many hats in a smaller organization, but this should not cause any problems as long as responsibilities and authorities are known. The identification of the functions that have the responsibility and authority to identify nonconformities and handle corrective and preventive action are especially important in the quality management system. Many times the responsibilities and authorities of the members of an organization are shown through the organization's structure, which may be documented through the use of an organization chart.

Required and Suggested Documents

No documents are required but you may want to consider the use of organization charts and job descriptions.

 Techniques for Small and Medium Businesses

Determine how the organization is going to define and communicate the responsibilities and authorities.
Explain the system used to define and communicate the responsibilities and authorities in the quality manual.

5.5.2 Management Representative

The responsibility and authority for the quality management program needs to be centrally controlled. This control needs to be near the top of any organization or the emphasis on quality is liable to suffer. As a result, the standard requires that the organization place this responsibility and authority in the hands of a "management representative." This management representative must be part of the top layer of management. Like any other job, the standard does not require the duties of the management representative to be performed by one person.

The management representative is responsible for putting the quality management system in place and keeping it effective and up to date. The representative is responsible for reporting the status of the program to management and making sure that the entire organization is customer-focused.

 Techniques for Small and Medium Businesses

Experience has shown that the management representative is usually:

- The person in charge of the facility when there are less than 20 employees

- Either the person in charge of the facility or a direct report when there are 21 to 50 employees

- A direct report to the facility manager when there are 51 to 250 employees

Usually the facility manager or a direct report is assigned the role of alternate management representative, who assumes responsibility in the absence of the designated management representative. Keep in mind that the management representative can have other duties.

5.5.3 Internal Communication

Poor communications can be a major source of problems in many businesses and quality management systems. This is why the standard addresses this concept as a management responsibility. The management of the organization must establish a culture of open communications to assure an effective quality management system.

Techniques for Small and Medium Businesses

In most businesses, frequent interaction naturally promotes communication. If this is the situation in your business, utilize it as your system for internal communication. Smaller businesses have an advantage over larger businesses in this area. If you do not have open informal communication, you will have to develop a more formal system.

Good form (for example, sales order, purchase order) design and development will also promote effective internal communication.

In many small and medium businesses, each employee may have more than one basic job responsibility and may also be cross trained to take over responsibilities and authorities when the need arises. This also promotes good internal communications.

5.6 MANAGEMENT REVIEW

5.6.1 General

Management is required to regularly review your quality management system, the frequency of which depends upon the maturity of your system. Early in the implementation process, the reviews should be rather frequent so that management can react quickly to problems. As your system matures, the interval can be lengthened. Never wait more than a year for a management review. Monthly or quarterly management reviews are more effective in reaping the benefits of your quality management system.

Management reviews are performed to make sure that the quality management system continues to be suitable, adequate, and effective. The review looks for needed changes to the quality management system and for improvement opportunities. As we said earlier, the quality policy and the quality objectives need to be evaluated during these reviews to make sure that they are current and do not need to be modified or improved.

Required and Suggested Documents

You may want a documented procedure for performing management reviews.

Required Records

Results of the management review must be recorded. The management review records must be controlled.

 Techniques for Small and Medium Businesses

Many smaller businesses use either minutes of the management review meetings or a summary report of the meetings to serve as the record of the management reviews.

5.6.2 Review Input

One of your first agenda items should be follow-up actions from previous management reviews. Customer feedback is second, both positive and negative.

Next, look at the input from your audit results, along with the status of your corrective and preventive actions. Finally, look at process performance and product conformity data.

Do not forget to look inward and evaluate what changes have occurred in your business that might affect your quality management system. Also, do not forget to ask for recommendations for improvement.

 Techniques for Small and Medium Businesses

You need to look at follow-up items from your previous management reviews, determine whether or not the action items have been completed, and verify that the actions were effective. The frequency, magnitude, success in implementation, time required for implementation, and other measures of your preventive and corrective actions will show you where you may need to modify or improve your quality management system.

Customer feedback lets you know how well you are meeting customers' product requirements and where you may have problems with your marketing, sales, delivery, customer service, and other customer-related processes.

Process performance data and product conformity data are obtained from your major production and quality records and from nonconformance reports. These serve to highlight where your product realization processes need improvement. Internal audits, which tell you where your quality management system is working and where it needs to be improved, are discussed under subclause 8.2.2.

All of these concepts are reactions to something that has occurred. You and your organization may come up with other ideas that you feel will improve your quality management system. These may come from discussions, reading about successes in other organizations, or new ideas. These need to be included in your management review.

5.6.3 Review Output

Management reviews are held to improve your quality management system. Therefore, the primary output from the meetings should be the decisions and actions identified to improve the effectiveness of the quality management system and processes. Product improvement, resource needs, and improved attainment of customer requirements are also important outputs of the management reviews. Do not forget to record these outputs.

Techniques for Small and Medium Businesses

Smaller businesses sometimes want to skip this step, along with the entire management review process, because they feel that it is not necessary when they can see and feel what is going on. But, *do not* skip this process step. Perform formal management reviews, which will enhance your organization and probably even the bottom line.

Be sure to act on the follow-up activities identified during your review. Do not allow them to be forgotten until the next review, because that means you do not have an effective quality management system and would probably not pass a registration audit.

Chapter 4

ANSI/ISO/ASQ Q9001–2000 Clause 6 Resource Management

6.1 PROVISION OF RESOURCES

Your organization needs resources to produce your product and plan, implement, and improve your quality management system. ANSI/ISO/ASQ Q9001–2000 is customer-focused. By adopting the standard, you have committed to improving customer satisfaction, and that means you need resources to meet customer requirements, including product requirements.

The resources being discussed are those needed for your entire quality management system, not just those necessary to produce a product. These resources, then, include those necessary to design, develop, and manage the quality management system; manage resources; provide for product realization; and measure, analyze, and improve the quality management system.

Resources include personnel, supplies, materials, equipment, facilities, and time. You'll notice that all of these resources, except one, are tangible physical resources. However, time is sometimes the most difficult resource for management to provide. Resources also include temporary and permanent personnel; both purchased and leased equipment and facilities; and, in most cases, subcontracted services.

6.2 HUMAN RESOURCES

6.2.1 General

Personnel that perform work affecting product quality must be competent on the basis of appropriate education, training, skills, and experience. Does this mean that only people making a product and inspecting it need to be qualified? No. What types of jobs might affect product quality? Virtually any job within any business will have a possible effect on quality. These include personnel involved in top management, resource management, product realization, support services, and the measurement-analysis-improvement processes.

For example, finance personnel handle invoicing, which is part of your product. Building maintenance personnel may inadvertently damage product or discard important paperwork while performing their work. In some way, virtually every employee can affect product quality.

6.2.2 Competence, Awareness, and Training

How do you ensure competent employees? First your organization must determine the necessary competence requirements for personnel. In large organizations, this is often accomplished with job descriptions, which define job skills; competency requirements; or similar requirements documents. Such detail is generally not necessary for small and medium organizations. In fact, it may be unnecessarily bureaucratic. Simple techniques that have been used are a brief table of minimum skill, training, and education requirements or a brief paragraph explaining these requirements. These documents are usually only one to two pages in length for the entire organization. Even these techniques are not necessary for smaller businesses where management is in routine contact with the entire work force. In these cases, management, and usually everyone, knows what the position requirements are.

Once your organization has determined what competencies are necessary, they need to provide the training or take other actions to satisfy these needs. The first step is to compare the competency requirements with the actual competencies of your employees. From this data you can develop a training plan for your organization. Training can be performed in-house or at external facilities such as seminars, institutions providing adult education, or similar facilities. Internal training can be performed by your own qualified personnel or by qualified personnel brought in to provide specific training.

After the training has been provided, you need to determine its effectiveness. There are several techniques that can be used. You should initially evaluate the effectiveness of training immediately after it is given, and then again later to determine how well the training was understood and retained. This evaluation may be formal, such as written or oral tests. Or, the trainers and management can talk with the trainees and evaluate the effectiveness of the training.

Your personnel must be aware of the relevance and importance of their activities and how they contribute to the achievement of your quality objectives. Many times this is performed at the implementation of the quality management system for current employees. New employees are given the same training along with other new employee training subjects, such as work rules, safety procedures, and so on.

You must maintain records of education, training, skills, and experience. In most organizations this is kept in personnel folders. Primary documentation of education, training, skills, and experience usually consists of the original job application of the employee or the employee's resume. When an employee receives additional training or education, this information needs to be added to the employee's record. You should also document on-the-job training given to provide new skills. Similarly, you need to update the record if the employee becomes certified in special skills, such as auditing or welding.

Required and Suggested Documents

There are no required documents, but you may want to document job descriptions, job skill requirements, training plans, or similar management tools.

Required Records

You must maintain appropriate records of education, experience, training, and qualification.

 Techniques for Small and Medium Businesses

- Determine if you want to document job requirements

- Evaluate your employees' competencies against job requirements

- Determine if you need to update your employees' records based on your knowledge of their skills, training, education, and experience

- Document this existing training

- Develop a training plan

- Provide the training

- Evaluate the effectiveness of the training

- Document the new training

6.3 INFRASTRUCTURE

What is infrastructure? Infrastructure is everything that your organization needs to produce and deliver the product or service:

- Buildings

- Workspace

- Utilities

- Process equipment

- Supporting services (such as buildings or equipment)

- Software maintenance

- Transportation and related equipment and facilities

- Communication (telephone, Internet, and Web services, including information technology support)

The only thing that it does not include is personnel.

 Techniques for Small and Medium Businesses

Most smaller businesses should not have to establish special systems for handling infrastructure; usually they work with existing facilities, equipment, and support services. When smaller businesses make any significant changes to their infrastructure, they go through an evaluation process that is unique to the anticipated change. The planning behind these changes usually involves most of the management of the organization. Therefore, the best way to handle this concept for the small and medium business quality manual is to stipulate that:

- The business will use the existing infrastructure

- The infrastructure will be examined during management reviews

- Changes to the infrastructure will be handled on a case-by-case basis

---

6.4 WORK ENVIRONMENT

Your organization has to determine and manage the *work environment* which is defined as the environment needed to achieve conformity to product requirements.

ANSI/ISO/ASQ Q9000–2000 defines work environment as the set of conditions under which work is performed, including physical, social, psychological, and environmental factors (such as temperature, recognition schemes, ergonomics, and atmospheric composition).

This requirement includes the concepts of:

• Clean rooms for electronic assembly operations

• Sterile environments for certain medical and medical device operations

• Refrigerated areas for some food handling and processing operations

• Air conditioning for some warehouse and manufacturing operations

• Special hyperbaric atmospheres and pressures in chambers used for special medical treatments

• Air conditioning for hospital, restaurant, and other types of service operations

• Special atmospheres for unique heat-treating operations

• Ergonomic workstations for employees performing repetitive operations

 Techniques for Small and Medium Businesses

The smaller business can handle the requirements for this subelement similar to the way that it can handle the requirement for infrastructure, by stating in the quality manual that:

• The business plans to use the existing work environments

• The work environments will be examined during management reviews

• Changes in work environment will be handled on a case-by-case basis

Chapter 5

ANSI/ISO/ASQ Q9001–2000 Clause 7 Product Realization

7.1 PLANNING OF PRODUCT REALIZATION

What is product realization? The term *product realization* is used more in Europe than in the United States. Product realization for our purposes is all of the processes needed to supply your product to your customer, from marketing and sales through manufacturing (for hardware) to delivery.

This clause is one of the more important clauses of ANSI/ISO/ASQ Q9001–2000. Subclause 4.1 "General requirements" established the requirement for you to plan your entire quality management system. Clause 8 "Measurement, analysis, and improvement," which we will discuss later, establishes the requirement for you to measure and improve the effectiveness of your quality management system. This clause (7.1) requires you to plan and develop your realization processes. These are all of the processes that:

- Result in a delivered product that conforms to customer requirements

- Improve customer satisfaction

- Encourage continual improvement

The planning of your product realization starts out with establishing the quality objectives for your product. These quality objectives are the broad objectives that we discussed under element 5.3 earlier. Next, determine what the specific requirements of the product are, and determine the criteria for product acceptance. Decide if you need to establish processes and documents specific to the product. Also, establish the verification, validation, monitoring, inspection, and testing activities specific to your product.

Don't forget records. Decide what records are necessary to provide proof that the product and the realization process meet requirements.

Optional Documented Procedures

You may want to develop and document a procedure describing how the planning of the realization process is achieved.

Required Records

The standard does not specify any records in particular. However, it does require you to define the records required to provide confidence of process and product conformity. Individual possible records are discussed for various subelements in this section.

 Techniques for Small and Medium Businesses

For most smaller businesses, meeting requirements of this element should not be difficult. In many cases the product or service is well-established and the quality objectives and requirements of the product are well-known. Except in rare instances, it will not be necessary to establish new or additional processes or documents. The resources specific to the product have already been established and usually no additional resources are necessary. Verification, validation, monitoring, inspection, and test activities are in place, and the criteria for product acceptance have also been established. In some cases, additional records may be needed to provide the evidence that the process and products fulfill the requirements in the specifications. For simple products and services the product

Continued

realization processes can be described concisely in the quality manual. It should not be necessary to include extensive details in the procedures.

If the product realization process is more complex it can be handled in one of two ways: (1) the process for a repetitive product can be described in the quality manual, augmented by procedures for some of the processes in a procedure manual when necessary; or (2) if the product or the processes are complex, it may be necessary to use quality plans. Quality plans are described in ANSI/ISO/ASQ Q9000–2000 as documents that describe how the quality management system is applied to a specific product, project, or contract. If needed, they can be as brief as a checklist or flowchart, which may reference existing documents. However, complex activities may require more detailed quality plans. ISO 10005: *Quality management—Guidelines for quality plans* is an excellent resource for guidance on developing quality plans if you do not already have your own process. ISO 10005 is one of the support documents for the 1994 series of ISO 9000 standards.

In summary, you should:

- Examine your product realization processes

- Examine your present process documentation, as applicable

- Determine if you need any additional process

- Determine if you need additional process documentation

- Evaluate your process record system

- Evaluate your product record system

- Determine if you need to modify your records system or add additional records

- Determine if you need to add additional resources

7.2 CUSTOMER-RELATED PROCESSES

7.2.1 Determination of Requirements Related to the Product

Product requirements start out with those specified by the customer, including delivery and post-delivery requirements, such as installation and servicing. These customer product requirements are usually relatively easy to obtain for routine, off-the-shelf items and catalog products. Customer requirements are also easy to obtain for services found in product service, product repair, restaurant, banking, and insurance types of businesses. Records related to these requirements are usually paper forms or computer data programs and files. In both cases, data control can be maintained by requiring certain blanks in the forms to be completed or requiring data to be entered into specific fields. Businesses operating in situations like this should not need any documented procedures for determining customer requirements.

Customer requirements for complex products and services, such as design and development, create a need for a more complex system. You need to have a system that will:

- Determine the customer's stated original product requirements

- Enable these requirements to be evaluated by your organization's personnel, such as engineering

- Probably enable discussions between your engineering and development personnel and specific individuals in your customer's organization

- Enable the determination of the final product requirements, allowing for controlled changes in these requirements

You also need to determine requirements that are not stated by the customer but are necessary for the use of the product. For example, if you manufacture light bulbs, it is up to you to know how thick the glass should be in order for the customer to be able to handle the bulb and screw it into a socket.

Since you, the provider of a product or service, are generally considered to be an expert in your field it is necessary for you to note the statutory and regulatory requirements related to your product or service. Many times these are requirements that your customer will have no knowledge of. In such cases, this determination is entirely up to your organization.

You will probably want to add requirements of your own. Examples include requirements that improve the desirability of your product or that make your product easier to produce.

Optional Documented Procedures

You may want to consider documenting the procedure used to determine what the product requirements are. This should only be necessary when you have complex products or processes.

Recommended Records

You should maintain records documenting what the customer requirements are.

You should include all written documents. You should also seriously consider documentation of oral communications of customer requirements. Although this is not a stated record requirement for an ISO 9001 system, many companies save a lot of time and money by having these records.

 Techniques for Small and Medium Businesses

Evaluate your procedures for determining customer requirements and determine what type of procedure documentation is necessary, if any. Evaluate your record system and see if it needs to be changed. If you are satisfied with your current system, as most small and medium businesses usually are, briefly describe your customer requirements system in your quality manual.

7.2.2 Review of Requirements Related to the Product

Your organization needs to review the requirements related to your product before you commit to supplying a product to the customer. You must perform the review prior to quoting on the product or contract, submitting a tender, accepting a contract or order, or accepting changes to contracts or orders. When you perform this review, you must make sure that:

- Product requirements are defined

- Contract or order requirements differing from those previously quoted or expressed are resolved

- Your organization has the ability to meet the defined requirements

If your customer does not provide a documented statement of requirements, your organization must confirm the requirements, usually verbal, before it accepts the order. Usually this confirmation is written; however, this may not always be the case. For example, a worker in a serving line at a cafeteria may just put the food on the customer's plate. If product changes are made, your organization has to make sure that relevant documents are changed or amended, and that affected personnel are made aware of the change in requirements.

The individuals or groups that perform these reviews will differ depending upon the type of product or service being offered. For example, a clerk may do an order review if the customer is buying a catalog item. The purpose of the clerical review is to make sure that the catalog item is correctly identified. The actual review of the product would be made when it was included in the catalog.

On the other hand, many individuals or groups, such as engineering, sales, service delivery, or manufacturing, may be involved if the product is a large software development project, major construction project, major design project, or complex physical product.

Optional Documented Procedures

You may want to develop a procedure for the review of customer requirements.

Required Records

The standard requires that you maintain and control records of the results of the review of customer requirements and subsequent follow-up actions.

 Techniques for Small and Medium Businesses

Experience has shown that clerical personnel perform this review for simple or repetitive products. The review usually includes at least one member of top management when the product is complex or large. This is an area where some smaller businesses have problems. When they first start out, the owner or manager deals directly with the customer and the review is effective. However, errors and omissions start to occur when the business grows and others deal directly with the customer. Review your system and, if it is not a source of errors, describe it in your quality manual. If you are having problems, you should revise your system to minimize the errors and then describe it in your quality manual.

7.2.3 Customer Communication

You need to have an effective system for communicating with your customers. Obviously this relates to communications regarding your product, especially in the areas of inquiries, quotes, orders, and contracts. However, you need an equally effective system (or possibly more complex system) for handling changes. Perhaps not so obvious is the need for an effective system for handling customer feedback, both positive and negative. The extent of the customer communications process should depend on the size of your business and how complex your customer communications are.

Optional Documented Procedures

You may want to have a procedure for customer communications.

Recommended Records

You may want to have a journal to write down customer feedback, including positive statements, suggestions, questions, and customer complaints. If a journal is not adequate for your needs, you may want to develop a form for all members of your organization to use for documenting customer comments. Such records might come in handy when you measure customer satisfaction under element 8.2.1 "Customer satisfaction."

Techniques for Small and Medium Businesses

This is an area where most smaller businesses have an advantage. Usually the people within a small organization are close to the customer, and feedback is received by top management rather quickly. Many times top management hears customer complaints and positive comments directly from the customer. In larger organizations, it is sometimes necessary to establish formal feedback systems in order for top management to be aware of customer concerns and other feedback.

Evaluate your customer feedback system to determine if it needs to be formalized and if you want it documented. Managers can do this easily with log, diary, or journal entries, which help them review customer feedback during management reviews.

7.3 DESIGN AND DEVELOPMENT

7.3.1 Design and Development Planning

Design and development planning is necessary, but only to the level of detail required to meet your design objectives. You do not want to generate unnecessary paperwork.

You need to plan and control the design and development of your product. Your planning must cover the stages of your design and development processes; your review, verification, and validation activities pertinent to your design and development stages; and the responsibilities and authorities for your design and development activities.

Your organization has to manage the interfaces between different groups involved in the design and development efforts to make sure that there is effective communication and clear assignment of responsibility. Don't forget to update your planning as design and development progresses.

Flowcharts, as we have discussed before, are an effective planning tool. Gantt and PERT charts are also extremely effective graphical tools for design planning. These tools can be updated as your projects advance, which makes it easy to keep track of the stages of your design and development. Expanded versions of these tools can be used to show responsibilities and authorities. These tools can also be used to identify the review, verification, and validation activities.

There are various groups within your organization that may be involved in the design and development of your products, including research and development, marketing and sales, purchasing, quality assurance and quality management, engineering, materials technology, production/manufacturing, service groups, facilities management, warehouse, logistics, transportation, communications, and information systems. All of these functions do not necessarily have to be included in the designing and development of a product. However, in most organizations, two or more of these functions are involved. Design planning is not limited to just research and development or design and development groups.

Interfaces outside of your organization include your customer, of course, and also may include subcontractors, regulatory bodies, and industry associations. Your interface planning should include: what information is to be received and transmitted between groups, the purpose of the information being transmitted, the transmittal mechanisms to be used, and records maintenance requirements.

Optional Documented Procedures

You determine the type of documentation required for your product or project plan. Organizations with simple design systems and repetitive products that have short design cycle times may just briefly describe their design and development planning systems in their quality manual. On the other hand, if your organization is involved in designing and developing complex products or projects, you should document your current effective design system now. If you do not have an effective design and development planning system, you need to develop one to assure customer satisfaction, reduce your costs, and improve profits.

Recommended Records

You determine what design and development records should be maintained. Your records will depend upon the complexity and mix of your products.

 Techniques for Small and Medium Businesses

Many small and medium businesses will have a relatively simple design process and therefore the design planning will be minimal. Frequently the designer in a smaller business will have design responsibility as one of many tasks. In many cases

Continued

the primary design responsibility is to modify current designs to new uses. In these situations the design planning can be briefly described in the quality manual rather than having to develop a design plan for each new product. Sometimes this design work can be accomplished in half a day and, as might be expected, the interfaces involved are also minimal.

7.3.2 Design and Development Inputs

Obviously the functional and performance requirements are necessary for any design, which can be obtained directly from the customer in the case of uniquely designed products. Marketing is the source of this information for commercial products or products made to meet a market need.

Statutory and regulatory requirements come from government bodies where the product is being manufactured, transported, or used. Sometimes your customer can furnish this information. However, if the customer is not aware of these requirements, it is your responsibility as a product designer to determine what these requirements are. Other sources of these types of design requirements can be industry product standards that you choose to follow either because of interchangeability or because they are customer or legal requirements.

In some instances design requirements will come from previous similar designs. This occurs when you modify an old product to improve it, or develop a slightly different new product for another application. Using information from an old design can significantly reduce the time required to produce new designs. You also need to include other requirements that are necessary for the design and development of the product.

You need to then review all of these design inputs to make sure that they are complete and adequate. You also need to make sure that these requirements are unambiguous and not in conflict with each other. Ambiguous and conflicting requirements can cause many problems in designing and producing products and services. These problems include unnecessary redesign and remanufacturing expenses.

Optional Documented Procedures

You may want to develop a procedure that defines what type of information will be written down to make sure that the product requirements are known and documented. The procedure should define the review process to assure that requirements are adequate and complete.

Required Records

The standard stipulates that records of the design input requirements must be maintained.

Techniques for Small and Medium Businesses

You can use a journal, or perhaps a sheet of paper in your product design file, to record the product design requirements when your design efforts are minimal. Make the records fit the needs of your business. If more detailed records are necessary, then by all means develop them.

7.3.3 Design and Development Outputs

Your design process is going to have an output that enables you to provide your product or service. You have to be able to compare this design output to your design input requirements. You have to make sure that your design and development output:

- Meets the design and development input requirements

- Provides the information necessary for purchasing materials, supplies, and services

- Provides the information that you need to produce the product or provide the service

- Allows you to determine acceptability of the product and service

- Specifies the characteristics of the product that are fundamental for its safe and proper use

The output from your design and development efforts must be processed through the approval process before the output is released. This is done by making sure that you have followed your design plan and all other aspects of your design process before you release the design for production or deliver the design to your customer.

Examples of design output include:

- Engineering—drawings and calculations

- Fashion—sketches and material specs

- Graphics—final layout for publication

- Food product—recipe

- Legal practice—legal advice

- Advertising agency—marketing campaign

Required and Suggested Documents

Your organization's design outputs must be provided in a form that allows you to verify it against the design and development inputs.

Optional Documented Procedures

You may want to develop a procedure that describes the content and form of the design output.

 Techniques for Small and Medium Businesses

Existing businesses performing design usually have an approval process in place and their design output documented in some manner. Therefore you should be able to just document your design output process in your quality manual and make modifications if necessary.

7.3.4 Design and Development Review

You need to perform systematic reviews of your design and development to evaluate the ability of the design results to meet requirements, identify any problems, and propose actions. Participants in these reviews must include representatives of functions concerned with the design and development stages being reviewed. These functions, including your customers, were discussed earlier.

The following list identifies some concepts you may want to consider when conducting your design reviews:

- Items pertaining to customer needs and satisfaction—

  - Comparison of customer needs expressed in the product brief with technical specifications for materials, products, and processes

  - Validation of the design through prototype tests

  - Ability to perform under expected conditions of use and environment

  - Considerations of unintended uses and misuses

  - Safety and environmental compatibility

  - Compliance with regulatory requirements, national and international standards, and corporate practices

  - Comparisons with competitive design

  - Comparison with similar designs, especially analysis of internal and external problem history to avoid repeating problems

- Items pertaining to product specification and service requirements—

  - Reliability, serviceability, and maintainability requirements

  - Permissible tolerances and comparison with process capabilities

- Product acceptance/rejection criteria

- Installability, ease of assembly, storage needs, shelf life, and disposability

- Benign failure and fail-safe characteristics

- Aesthetic specifications and acceptance criteria

- Failure modes and effects analyses, and fault tree analysis

- Ability to diagnose and correct problems

- Labeling, warnings, identification, traceability requirements, and user instructions

- Review and use of standard parts

- Items pertaining to process specifications and service requirements—

  - Manufacturability of the design, including special process needs

  - Mechanization, automation, assembly, and installation of components

  - Capability to inspect and test the design, including special inspection and test requirements

  - Specification of materials, components, and subassemblies, including approved supplies and suppliers as well as availability

  - Packaging, handling, storage, and shelf life requirements, especially safety factors relating to incoming and outgoing items

Optional Documented Procedures

You may want to define and document the process for the design review, including who is responsible for conducting it, the participants that should be involved, what is to be covered, the records to be kept, and the requirements for the follow-up actions.

Required Records

The results of the reviews and subsequent follow-up actions have to be recorded. The records must be controlled. You should consider including who was included in the design review, who conducted it, and its content.

Techniques for Small and Medium Businesses

Design reviews in smaller businesses need to include all affected functions, including the customer when necessary. They can be conducted in a meeting or the various functions involved can review the design output individually. However, these reviews do not need to be a documentation nightmare. Records may consist of meeting minutes, journal entries, or notes in a design file.

7.3.5 Design and Development Verification

When you verify the design you are using data to make sure that the specified requirements have been met. Some techniques that have been used for design verification include:

- Comparing a new design with a similar proven design
- Using alternative calculations or methodologies
- Performing qualification tests
- Reviewing the design documents before release

In some instances a verification process may be specified by an external source. These verification procedures may come from industry, national, or international standards. These verification procedures may also be stipulated by a regulatory agency.

Optional Documented Procedures

You may want to consider defining the verification process in a procedure indicating:

- Who performs the verification

- When the verification is to be performed

- How the verification is to be performed

- How the verification is to be documented

- How the follow-up and reverification actions are to be handled

Required Records

The results of the verification and subsequent follow-up actions must be recorded. These records must be controlled.

Techniques for Small and Medium Businesses

In actual practice, most smaller businesses use one or more of the techniques mentioned above. Their choice is based on what has proven successful in their line of business. You should:

- Evaluate your present design verification techniques and record system

- Determine if they need to be modified or can be left as is

- Describe your design verification system in your quality manual

7.3.6 Design and Development Validation

Validation is checking to see if the product works. Sometimes it is not possible to perform a design validation until a product is delivered and put into use. However, design validation can be accomplished by validating units of the design separately.

Optional Documented Procedures

You should consider defining the validation process in a procedure including:

- Who performs the validation

- When the validation is to be performed

- How the validation is to be performed

- How the validation is to be documented

- If and when partial validations should be performed

- How the follow-up and revalidation actions are to be handled

Required Records

The results of the validation and subsequent follow-up actions must be recorded. The records must be controlled.

 Techniques for Small and Medium Businesses

As with verification, most smaller businesses have determined what is successful for them and what is not. Therefore you should:

- Evaluate your present design validation techniques and record system

- Determine if they need to be modified or not

- Describe your design validation system in your quality manual

If you feel that it would be beneficial, you may document your design validation procedures.

7.3.7 Control of Design and Development Changes

Problems with design and development changes can cause headaches in many organizations when design and development changes are not handled properly. Your system must identify and record design and development changes.

You must review, validate, and verify design and development changes, as appropriate, including an evaluation of the effect of the changes on the component parts and the product that has already been delivered.

You must also approve design and development changes before implementing them.

What are some of the valid reasons for design changes?

- Your customer requests a change

- A supplier or subcontractor requests a change

- You want to improve the function or performance of the product or service

- There are changes made to safety, regulatory, or other requirements

- Corrective or preventive action necessitates a change

- Design review, design verification, or design validation identifies changes that need to be made while the design is in process

There also are other reasons for design changes. These are real life reasons that occur because our world isn't perfect. Some examples are:

- Omissions or errors identified after the completion of the design

- Manufacturing and/or installation difficulties that are discovered after the design phase

Required and Suggested Documents

ANSI/ISO/ASQ Q9001–2000 requires that design and development changes be documented in the design output documents.

Optional Documented Procedures

You may want to document your change control procedure, making sure that:

- Changes are communicated to all functions and individuals involved

- Documentation related to changes is both adequate and controlled

- Authorization is obtained and documented for changes

Required Records

The standard requires records of the results of the review of design and development changes and any necessary actions.

 Techniques for Small and Medium Businesses

Most successful smaller businesses have a design change and review process in place that includes the maintenance of records. However, there is a problem that many small and medium businesses must watch out for. There's a tendency to bypass documentation because of the ease of informal communication. This lack of communication results in the change not being completed.

Review your design change procedure. If it is being followed, meets the requirements of ANSI/ISO/ASQ Q9001–2000, and is not causing any problems, you should continue using it and briefly describe it in your quality manual. However, if you are having problems you should modify your design change process to meet the requirements of your business and ANSI/ISO/ASQ Q9001–2000.

7.4 PURCHASING

7.4.1 Purchasing Process

You are responsible for the quality of the material, supplies, and services that go into your product. Unless you are mining the material, you are purchasing something that will affect your product.

You are responsible for making sure that the material, supplies, products, and services that you buy for your products conform to specified purchase requirements. The type and extent of control that you apply to your supplier and the purchased product depends upon the effect that the purchased product will have on subsequent production processes or the final product. For example, if you are buying bulk salt for use on wintertime roadways, you probably would not be as concerned about minor contamination than if you were buying sea salt to be used in a gourmet recipe. Likewise, you would not be as concerned about the quality of a bolt holding a minor subassembly in a lawnmower than the quality of the castle nut mounting the wheel to the axle.

You are responsible for evaluating and selecting suppliers based on their ability to provide a product that meets your requirements. You must establish criteria for the selection and evaluation of these suppliers. The standard gives you wide latitude in establishing this criteria and focuses on the requirement that the purchased product meets your stated specifications. The standard does require, however, that you maintain records of your supplier evaluations and any necessary actions arising from those evaluations.

Optional Documented Procedures

You should consider having a procedure that describes the process and defines the criteria for the selection and evaluation of suppliers.

Required Records

You must record the results of evaluations and follow-up actions. Usually these records contain the results of supplier evaluations, corrective actions requested of the suppliers, and the results of those corrective actions.

 Techniques for Small and Medium Businesses

Supplier records and evaluations may be documented in a diary or log. Problems with nonconforming or defective product, off-schedule delivery, and quality system problems are some of the primary evaluation criteria used by businesses. Although not required by the standard, a useful technique for some businesses is to use an approved supplier list backed up by supplier data files.

7.4.2 Purchasing Information

You need to describe the product or service that you want from your supplier. This can be as simple as the identification of a catalog number or a 60-page contract that may describe:

- The product in extreme detail, including design fit, form, function, and performance requirements

- Specifications applicable to the product

- Requirements for qualification of personnel and/or equipment

- Requirements for approval of product

- Requirements for approval of procedures

- Requirements for approval of processes

- Requirements for approval of equipment

- Supplier quality management system requirements

You have to make sure that you have adequately specified purchase requirements before you submit them to your supplier. Again, this depends upon the complexity of the product that you are ordering. This may amount to signing or initialing a purchase order for a simple product. It could also mean using a multistage purchasing document package review process for such products as specialized software packages, business administration services, major manufacturing equipment, or complex subassemblies.

Optional Documented Procedures

You should consider developing a procedure that details what information needs to be included in purchasing documents. The procedure should include the approval process or processes to be used before the purchase document is released to the supplier.

Recommended Records

Although the standard does not require that copies of the purchase documents must be maintained, you should consider keeping them to provide evidence that the proper material has been ordered. If your purchase order review process is complex, you should consider keeping records of the review.

 Techniques for Small and Medium Businesses

Evaluate your current system for making purchases. If it meets your requirements and the requirements of ANSI/ISO/ASQ Q9001–2000, describe the system in your quality manual and continue to use it. If you are experiencing problems, revise your system and describe the revised system in your quality manual. You should then evaluate your revised system during your next management review.

7.4.3 Verification of Purchased Product

Verification of purchased product addresses only the product that is used in or may have an effect on your product, it does not address supplies that are used in the operation of your business but do not affect the final product. Examples of products that would probably have no effect on your final product include office supplies and building maintenance supplies.

Some of the techniques used for verification of product include:

- Certification of your suppliers and their ability to meet your purchase requirements. You may do this yourself or you may choose to base this certification on registration to ANSI/ISO/ASQ Q9001–2000 or a similar quality management system. In this situation you may not require any inspection or test upon the receipt of the product.

- Performance of sampling inspection upon receipt of the product.

- Performance of a 100 percent inspection upon receipt of the product. In fact, you may do more than a 100 percent inspection.

- Verification of the product at your supplier's facility.

- A contract to have the verification performed by an independent source.

- Use of a combination of these verification techniques.

No matter what purchased product verification procedure you use, you need to make sure that it is effectively implemented. If you or your customer do choose to verify the product at your supplier's facility, you must state the planned verification arrangements and method for product release in your purchasing information.

Optional Documented Procedures

You may want to document the process used to verify purchased product. If you or your customer verify purchased product at the supplier's facility, you may want to describe the process in your quality manual.

Recommended Records

You should consider keeping records of product verification and release.

Techniques for Small and Medium Businesses

Evaluate your current system for verifying the purchased product. If it meets your requirements and the requirements of ANSI/ISO/ASQ Q9001–2000, describe the system in your quality manual and continue to use it. If you are experiencing problems, revise your system and describe the revised system in your quality manual. You should then evaluate your revised system during your next management review.

7.5 PRODUCTION AND SERVICE PROVISION

7.5.1 Control of Production and Service Provision

In order to provide a consistent product you need to provide services or produce a product under controlled conditions. There are many aspects of controlled conditions. ANSI/ISO/ASQ Q9001–2000 requires the inclusion of six areas of controlled conditions when they are applicable:

1. You must have information that describes the characteristics of the product. This is usually accomplished with final product and interim specifications when a physical product is involved. Examples would be in-process and final drawings for a bicycle, or in-process and final specifications for a bulk chemical compound. Even in service industries, such as sewing machine repair, furnace repair, computer repair, and other types of aftermarket repair operations, there is information that describes the characteristics of the product. The software industry has similar information that describes product characteristics.

2. Work instructions that tell employees how to perform tasks are necessary in some instances. Details of the work instructions depend upon the complexity of the task and the skills of the

employee. In a fast food restaurant you may need detailed instructions on how to cook and assemble a hamburger. In this case, the product is not complex but the employees are usually entry-level and untrained in cooking skills. On the other hand, the work instruction for a chef in a restaurant might just consist of a recipe. Similar situations exist in process and hardware industries, where an entry-level employee would need detailed instructions on how to operate equipment but a skilled operator might only need process control settings.

3. Suitable equipment is applicable in all process and manufacturing operations. This is even true for handmade products; early man needed the right type of stone to chip the flint to make arrows. Suitable equipment is also necessary in banking, insurance, hospital, medical, restaurant, school, and other types of service operations. Suitable equipment is obviously necessary in the software industry.

4. The availability and use of monitoring and measuring devices is necessary in some instances. Measuring devices are necessary in the machining industry. Monitoring devices are necessary in the chemical process and welding industries, as well as the food preparation business. However, monitoring devices are not usually necessary in the software and soft service industries, such as hotels, banks, and insurance.

5. The implementation of the monitoring and measuring activity is usually necessary. Monitoring and measuring, especially monitoring, does not necessarily require the use of equipment. Service delivery employees may be monitored and evaluated on their ability to provide the service. Management may also monitor in-service facilities such as grocery stores, where additional cashiers are assigned to checkout when the volume of customers increases.

6. Release, delivery, and post-delivery activities must be implemented. These activities differ from industry to industry: hardware and process industries may use classical inspection and test methods; a chef may use a taste test; a sweeper repairman may use a vacuum test; an airline pilot would use the preflight checklist; and equipment installation personnel might use checklists and

pilot runs. Systems to make these activities consistent must be established when these activities are used.

Required and Suggested Documents

The standard requires the availability of information that specifies the characteristics of the product, and, where necessary, the availability of work instructions. You should consider developing these documents if you do not already have them as part of your design output process or another process.

Optional Documented Procedures

The standard requires the implementation of defined processes for release, delivery, and applicable post-delivery activities. You should consider defining this process in a procedure or set of procedures.

 Techniques for Small and Medium Businesses

Most smaller businesses have systems that adequately meet these requirements. In some instances minor controls may need to be added.

Evaluate your production and/or service provision control systems. Do they meet the above requirements? Are the product characteristics adequately described? Do you have work instructions if and where they are necessary? Have your processes for the release, delivery, and post-delivery activities been implemented?

If they have, describe your current system in your quality manual. If you need to, make changes and then describe the revised system.

7.5.2 Validation of Processes for Production and Service Provision

This particular subelement is applicable when it is not possible to determine the conformance of a completed product to specified requirements. Hardware industry examples include welding, soldering, painting, heat-treating, casting, forging, and forming processes. Inspection techniques, such as ultrasonic testing and x-ray examination, also require validation of equipment, processes, and personnel. Service processes requiring validation include those producing financial and legal documents. The software industry must qualify personnel, equipment, and software development techniques.

The standard requires that you validate any processes for production and service operations where the resulting output cannot be verified by later monitoring or measurement, especially where deficiencies are seen only after the product is in use or the service has been delivered. Your validation of these processes must demonstrate their ability to achieve your planned results.

Your organization has to address the following concepts for these processes, when applicable:

- Specified criteria for review and approval of the processes

- Qualification or approval of equipment

- Qualification of personnel

- Use of specific methods and procedures

- Requirements for records

- Arrangements for revalidation, when necessary

Optional Documented Procedures

If your organization has "special processes" as previously described, you will probably have to prepare documents that define arrangements for validation that include, as applicable:

- Qualification of processes

- Qualification of equipment and personnel

- Use of defined methodologies and procedures

- Requirements for records

- Revalidation

Required Records

You need to define what records must be kept on process validation. Common records that are kept are usually records of equipment and personnel qualification when such records are applicable.

 Techniques for Small and Medium Businesses

Most smaller businesses that are involved in using these processes have already established their systems for process, equipment, and personnel qualification and validation. If this is your situation, briefly describe your system in your quality manual and refer to your current documentation and record systems. If your system for process validation is not already established, you'll need to develop it following these requirements.

7.5.3 Identification and Traceability

When it is applicable, your organization must identify your product using appropriate means throughout your product realization processes, including identification of the product status relative to monitoring and measurement requirements. In other words, you need to identify what the product is, if it has been inspected or not, and whether it has passed or failed the inspection. This may be accomplished by using records related to the product or marking the product itself.

When traceability is a requirement, you must control the unique identification of the product, which may be related to batches or lots of product or to individual parts or assemblies.

Optional Documented Procedures

You may want to consider a procedure defining your process for maintaining product identification and identifying the status of the product with respect to measurement and monitoring requirements.

If traceability is a requirement, you should develop a procedure describing this process.

Required Records

You need to define the records used for traceability if that is a requirement for your product. The standard requires that you must control and record the unique identification of the product, where traceability is a requirement. These records must be controlled.

 Techniques for Small and Medium Businesses

Again, most smaller businesses already have effective systems in place. If this is your situation, briefly describe your system for product identification in your quality manual. If traceability is a requirement, briefly describe your traceability system. If you already have documented procedures, refer to them in your quality manual.

7.5.4 Customer Property

You must take care of customer property when it is under your control or being used by your organization. You must identify, verify, protect, and safeguard customer property given to you for use or incorporation into your product. If any of your customer property is lost, damaged, or otherwise found to be unsuitable for use, you must report this to the customer and you must maintain records.

Examples of customer property are:

- Hardware—tools, instruments provided by customer for measurement purposes, and parts and assemblies to be used in a product

- Service—automobiles, appliances, and tools left for repair; film sent to a film processor; and training materials provided by your customer

- Process industries—chemicals to be included in the final product, material sent for heat-treating, pigment to be used in paint

- Software—source code

- Intellectual—designs, proprietary processes

Optional Documented Procedures

You may want to consider developing a procedure for the care of customer property depending on the nature of the customer property that you deal with.

Required Records

You are required to maintain records of any customer property that is lost, damaged, or otherwise found to be unsuitable for use. This record is for communication to your customer, but you should consider keeping a copy of this information for your own quality records.

 Techniques for Small and Medium Businesses

Most smaller businesses already have systems in place that meet the requirements for handling customer property, especially those in the service industry. Briefly describe your system in your quality manual.

7.5.5 Preservation of Product

The standard requires that you must preserve compliance during internal processing and delivery of the product to its intended destination. The preservation includes identification, handling, packaging, storage, and protection. The preservation also applies to the component parts of a product.

Your handling systems (including parts boxes, bins, pallets, conveyors, forklift trucks, and trucks used to transport the product) must keep the product from being damaged. In the process industry, pipelines are used to transport product and therefore would be included. If outside storage of your product is used, you must make sure that the product does not deteriorate. Handling systems also include packaging and marking for identification purposes. These are also addressed under this subelement.

Optional Documented Procedures

Depending on the nature of your product, you may want to document handling and storage procedures.

 Techniques for Small and Medium Businesses

Most smaller businesses usually have adequate systems in place to handle the preservation of their product. If this is your situation, briefly describe it in your quality manual.

7.6 Control of Monitoring and Measuring Devices

Under element 7.2.1 you determined product requirements. Now you need to provide evidence that your products conform to these requirements. In order to do this, you need to determine what measurements you need to make and what monitoring you need to perform, and use appropriate devices that are capable and stable. In some service industries and other businesses, measurement and monitoring equipment is not necessary.

If you need measurement and monitoring devices, you must determine what specific devices you need and establish processes for their use. You also need to make sure that this measurement and monitoring is carried out in a way that is consistent with the measurement and monitoring requirements that you have established.

Generally this means that your measurement equipment must be calibrated or verified at specified intervals or be calibrated prior to use. This calibration needs to be carried out against measurement standards traceable to national or international standards. Some measurements do not have a national or international standard that can be referenced. In these cases you must record the basis or foundation used for the calibration or verification of the device. In addition, your measuring and monitoring devices need to be adjusted or readjusted as necessary and be protected from adjustments that would nullify measurement results.

Your measuring and monitoring equipment must be identifiable so that the calibration status can be determined. Although there are numerous techniques to accomplish this, one of the most common is the use of calibration labels. Another is the use of serial numbers on the device that trace it to a calibration record. In situations where you have only one instrument of a kind, the record can state that it is for "blank" device without the use of a label or serial number. This technique was used for testing weights used for testing of cranes. The weights were made of steel plate filled with poured concrete. The weights were made in different tonnages and their identification was obvious.

The test weights mentioned above did not require much care to be protected from damage and deterioration during handling, maintenance, and storage. However, this protection is generally necessary for most monitoring and measuring devices.

When equipment is found that does not conform to requirements, you must assess and record the validity of previous measurement results and take appropriate action on the equipment. You must do the same for any product that was involved in possible erroneous measurements.

A measuring device can drift or wear over time. This is usually watched and the device is removed from service before it becomes inaccurate. If, however, the device is found to be just beyond the acceptance limit, any product that was produced since the last calibration is suspect. Check with the function responsible for establishing the original product specification to determine the consequence of a slightly out-of-specification product. Many times this specification writing body (for example, engineering and/or customer) determines that no further action is necessary. Sometimes product that was accepted on a go/no-go basis is measured using variables data and the distribution of the suspect product is examined. In other cases, truckloads of product have been recalled. The action that you need to take is determined by the degree and seriousness of the possibly nonconforming product erroneously accepted by the suspect measuring device.

The standard addresses computer software used in the monitoring and measurement of specified requirements. When such software is used, you must confirm the ability of the software to meet its intended application prior to the initial use of the software, and you must reconfirm the ability of the software as necessary.

ISO 10012-1 *Quality assurance requirements for measuring equipment—Part 1: Metrological confirmation systems for measuring equipment* and 10012-2 *Quality assurance for measuring equipment—Part 2: Guidelines for control of measurement processes* are recommended for measurement systems guidance and for the management of measurement and monitoring equipment.

Optional Documented Procedures

You should consider developing a procedure for the control of measuring and monitoring devices. The procedure should cover calibration requirements and storage and handling procedures.

Required Records

The standard requires that the results of the calibration be recorded. In addition, the basis used for calibration must be recorded in situations where no national or international standards exist. These records must be controlled.

Techniques for Small and Medium Businesses

Most smaller businesses have good calibration programs. If this is your situation, briefly describe your calibration program in your quality manual and refer to your present system documents and records.

Frequently, however, smaller businesses only check their measuring devices against one or two standards instead of performing a true calibration. If this is a possibility you should obtain copies of ISO 10012-1 and ISO 10012-2 and use them to evaluate your calibration program. This is definitely not a requirement but it should enable you to establish a calibration program that will help your organization improve.

Chapter 6

ANSI/ISO/ASQ Q9001–2000 Clause 8 Measurement, Analysis, and Improvement

8.1 GENERAL

A primary benefit of an ANSI/ISO/ASQ Q9001–2000 quality management program is its ability to improve the company's profitability, efficiency, and efficacy by using measurement and analysis to show where you can make improvements to your system. In order to gain these benefits, you must plan and implement monitoring, measuring, analysis, and improvement processes. These processes will also show that your products conform to product requirements and your quality management system conforms to your requirements and those of ANSI/ISO/ASQ Q9001–2000.

You must use statistical techniques in conjunction with measuring and monitoring systems to improve their effectiveness. Statistical techniques also are a powerful tool in data analysis. Just looking at data and information is a statistical technique. If you are in a small or medium business and only have one customer complaint in a year, the review of that complaint is a statistical analysis tool.

However, in most cases, we have much more data that we have to analyze. Just looking at a bunch of data is not a very effective analysis tool. Statistical techniques (especially graphics, which give a "picture" of the data) enable us to look at data in systematic ways.

ANSI/ISO/ASQ Q9001–2000 is intentionally silent on what techniques to use. As we have said throughout this text, your quality management system is unique to your organization. Therefore, only your organization can determine the most effective ways to meet the requirements of this clause.

Techniques for Small and Medium Businesses

ISO TC 176 developed ISO/TR 10017:1999 *Guidance on statistical techniques for ISO 9001:1994*, which may help you identify the many techniques that you can use for various elements of your quality management system. Although it was written for the 1994 edition of the standard, you should find it a useful guidance tool for an ANSI/ISO/ASQ Q9001–2000 quality management system.

Evaluate statistical techniques and see how you can use them in your business. An excellent text on the use of statistical tools is *SPC Tools for Everyone* by John T. Burr, published by ASQ Quality Press. Another helpful reference is ISO 11462-1:2000 *Guidelines for implementation of statistical process control (SPC)—Part 1: Elements of SPC.*

ISO/TR 10017:1999 identified 12 broad categories of statistical techniques. The more commonly used techniques are descriptive statistics, design of experiments, process capability analysis, sampling, statistical process control charts, and trend or time series analysis. The report also identified some additional, extremely effective techniques that, in the author's experience, are used less often in business and are generally harder to learn to use. These techniques are hypothesis testing, measurement analysis, regression, reliability analysis, simulation, and statistical tolerancing.

Continued

Most of the tools listed as common tools can be self-taught or taught in a group with facilitators. Design of experiments is included as a common tool, not because of its simplicity, but because it is widely used in some specific industries. You should take a design of experiments course if you want to learn how to use the tool effectively.

Table 6.1 describes the more frequently used statistical techniques.

Statistical techniques have various uses in the different elements of your quality management system. Table 6.3 on page 120 shows you the various reasons for using statistical techniques and the techniques that you can use for each clause and subclause of ANSI/ISO/ASQ Q9001–2000.

Table 6.1   Common statistical techniques for ISO 9001 programs.

Technique	Explanation
Easy graphical techniques	Pareto charts are used to tally data in descending or ascending frequency order. They are used to identify significant areas for investigation. Cause-and-effect or fishbone diagrams are used to tie multiple possible causes to a significant effect that is generally causing a problem. Cross plots are a form of visual regression used to identify changes in a dependent variable as a result of changes in an independent variable.
Descriptive statistics	Descriptive statistics are used to summarize numerical or quantitative data. The mean, median, or mode are usually used to describe central tendency. Range, standard deviation, or variance are used to show spread or dispersion. Pie charts, bar charts, histograms, and scatter plots are some of the simple graphical methods used to display descriptive statistics.
Design of experiments	Designed experiments are used to carry out tests or investigations in a planned manner. Statistical assessment techniques are then used to evaluate the data so that conclusions may be reached with certain levels of confidence. Design of experiments finds its greatest use in investigating complex systems where outcomes may be influenced by a larger number of factors.

Continued

Technique	Explanation
Process capability analysis	Process capability analyses are used to examine the variability of a process so that an estimate can be made of its ability to produce product that conforms to requirements.
Sampling	Sampling is a statistical method for obtaining information about a characteristic of a large group of data (population) by studying a smaller representative fraction (sample) of the population.
Statistical process control charts	Statistical process control charts graph data obtained from samples drawn from a process. The data are plotted in sequence. The statistical process control chart shows control limits based on the variability of the process when it is stable. The chart is then used to detect changes in the process.
Trend analysis	Trend analysis is also called time series analysis. Trend analyses are used for studying observations made sequentially in time, describing patterns in time series data, detecting a turning point in a trend, and identifying outliers or extreme values.

Source: Based on ISO/TR 10017:1999

8.2 MONITORING AND MEASUREMENT

8.2.1 Customer Satisfaction

You must monitor information relating to whether your customer thinks that you are fulfilling their requirements. You must determine the methods you are going to use for obtaining and using this information.

Each business is unique in its ability to obtain customer satisfaction information. Table 6.2 is a guide to possible sources for customer satisfaction information for your organization.

Optional Documented Procedures

You may want to have a procedure on how you are going to handle customer satisfaction. The procedure may cover the who, what, when, where, why, and how of:

- Gathering the information

- Analyzing the information

- Acting on the analysis

Table 6.2 Sources of customer satisfaction information.

(P = Primary S = Secondary T = Tertiary)

	Software	Service	Hardware	Processed Material
Communicating directly with customers	P	P	P	P
Customer complaints	P	P	P	P
Customer satisfaction studies	S	S	S	S
Focus groups	T	P	S	T
Questionnaires and surveys	S	S	P	S
Reports from consumer organizations	S	P	P	T
Reports in various media	P	S	P	T
Returns	P	S	P	P
Sector and industry studies	P	P	S	P
Software bugs	P	NA	NA	NA
Subcontracted collection and analysis of data	S	P	S	T
Warranty claims	S	S	P	T

 Techniques for Small and Medium Businesses

Remember that customer satisfaction is one of the primary reasons for having a quality management system. It is a prime focus of ANSI/ISO/ASQ Q9000–2000. This is an element of the quality management system that should be relatively easy for most small and medium businesses to comply with, because upper-level management is usually extremely close to the customer base. Your management probably has a pretty good "feel" for the customer's satisfaction.

Continued

The standard does not require any specific documentation in this area. In fact, in most cases, there is no need for a documented procedure. However, it would be helpful if you and your management would maintain diaries or journals of customer comments. This material can then be reviewed and analyzed for trends and possible areas of improvement. Of course, this material will also be used in your management reviews.

8.2.2 Internal Audit

You need to conduct internal audits to determine if your quality management system is doing what you want it to do and verify that it conforms to the requirements of ANSI/ISO/ASQ Q9001–2000. You must plan your audit program to make sure that it is effective. Some of the factors involved are:

- The status of the process to be audited—is it new or has it been in place for some time?

- The importance of the processes—what is the consequence of a failure?

- The status of the areas to be audited—are they stable?

- The importance of these areas—what is the effect of a failure on your product or business?

- The results of previous audit—where were the negative findings?

In planning your audit, you must determine the methods that you are going to use. There are many books on internal auditing, several of which are available from the American Society for Quality (ASQ). ISO also has the older quality management system audit standard series ISO 10011-1 through ISO 10011-3, and is currently developing a quality and environmental management system standard that should become ISO 19011 when it is completed. There are also many internal auditor training programs available from the American Society for Quality and others.

You must establish the scope of your audit. Audits do not need to cover your complete quality management system all at once. Perhaps you need to pay more attention in newly implemented areas, or you want to verify compliance to a particular set of criteria at one point in time. Only you can determine what areas and processes you need to audit with greater emphasis, and you also need to establish the criteria for each audit.

The frequency of your full and/or partial audits must also be decided. Again, newly implemented areas may need more frequent audits than older, established areas. Your audit schedule should be planned with your management review schedule in mind.

Your auditors must be objective and impartial during their audits. This does not mean that they must come from a different organization or a completely separate function within your organization. What this does mean, though, is that auditors must not audit their own work. Probably the greatest reason for this is that people cannot see their own errors, unintentional mistakes, and biases. However, owners and top managers of organizations have successfully performed internal audits when they have been able to distance themselves from the organization and perform the audit objectively.

Once the audit is complete, the management responsible for the audited area must make sure that actions are taken as soon as possible to eliminate nonconformances found and their causes. They must also make sure that follow-up is performed to verify that the nonconformances have been corrected and the causes have been eliminated. Reports of the verification results must be maintained.

Required Documented Procedure

You must have a documented procedure for internal audits that define the responsibilities and requirements for:

- Planning the audits

- Conducting the audits

- Reporting results and maintaining records

Required Records

The standard requires that you record the results of the audits.

Recommended Records

The standard requires that your periodic internal audits be used to determine whether the quality management system:

- Conforms to the requirements of the standard

- Has been effectively implemented and maintained

This means that you should have records that show that:

- The audit results have been reported to management

- Management has taken timely corrective action on deficiencies found during the audit

- Follow-up actions have included the verification of the implementation of corrective action

- The verification results have been reported

 Techniques for Small and Medium Businesses

Internal auditing is an extremely effective tool for the management of small and medium companies. Many times management in smaller organizations tends to rely upon their feel of the processes and how well they are working. A formal internal audit system will give concrete information on the true status of the organization and will result in improved operation of the organization.

Seek out some form of quality audit training for your organization. You can use texts, self-study courses, local organization courses, community colleges, or national training. Some communities have established mutual auditing groups where they train together and audit each other's organizations. See what resources you can find in your area.

8.2.3 Monitoring and Measurement of Processes

Even though this is an extremely short paragraph, it may take a lot of work to meet this requirement. This is not necessarily work in establishing a quality management system, although it could be. Product realization processes can require a large amount of measurement and monitoring on a regular basis. Throughout the standard you have been required to plan your processes. This element applies to the planning of the measurement and monitoring of processes to keep them under control.

The key to this element is to determine the important or major processes and process parameters that have the greatest impact on your product quality and your ability to meet your customer's requirements. Once these are determined, you must establish systems to monitor and control these processes so that your product continually meets its requirements. Production and inspection data analysis and the use of descriptive statistics and capability studies, which we discussed earlier, are excellent techniques to identify critical or important process parameters.

You are required to apply proper methods for monitoring and measuring these processes, the results of which must show that your processes have done what they are supposed to do. When these processes do not produce the correct results, you must:

- Correct the immediate problem, in other words, make a correction to the product as necessary to make sure the product conforms

- Take corrective action on the process to make sure that it is operating correctly and that the problem will not occur again

If you use manual monitoring and measurement techniques, you may want to record the results. However, if you have a closed loop control system or a device that monitors and records process parameters, you may not need to use a manual recordkeeping system. It is not even necessary that manual records be kept. It is up to you to determine what is in the best interest of your operation.

Optional Documented Procedures

The standard requires that you use suitable methods for measurement and monitoring of those realization processes necessary to meet customer requirements. These methods must confirm the continuing ability of each of your processes to satisfy its intended purpose. It is up to you to determine which processes you need to monitor, whether you need to have documented procedures for this determination, and how they will be monitored.

Recommended Records

The standard requires that you use suitable methods necessary for measurement and monitoring of the realization processes to meet customer requirements. These methods must confirm the continuing ability of each process to satisfy its intended purpose. It is up to you to determine what records you need to provide objective evidence that the processes and procedures have met customer requirements.

Techniques for Small and Medium Businesses

Most smaller businesses, especially those that have been in business for a long time, have identified their important process parameters and measurements. A good technique here is to examine your production and inspection records to identify areas where you have losses occurring. Study these losses and the parameters that contribute to them and make use of some of the statistical techniques discussed earlier. Identify process control parameters and monitoring techniques that you can use to control these process parameters.

You may be lucky and, like some organizations, have processes that easily meet product requirements. Either way, describe your basic process monitoring systems in your quality manual.

8.2.4 Monitoring and Measurement of Product

You are required to measure and monitor the characteristics of your product to make sure that it meets product requirements. Determine the measurements you need to make and at what stages in the product realization processes they should be performed. These measurements are done in accordance with the systems you set up under element 7.1 "Planning of product realization."

Typical areas of measurement begin with inspection and testing of materials that are used to make your product or perform your service. This was covered under element 7.4.3 "Verification of purchased product." The next area for measurement is the product realization process itself, which can vary from measuring vital signs such as temperature, blood pressure, and breathing rate in a medical service environment to measuring rough-turned diameters in a machining and grinding environment. The next, and sometimes final, area of measurement is on the completed product or service. These are the measurements, inspections, tests, and evaluations performed when the product or service is complete and about to be delivered to the customer. In cases where the product is not immediately delivered to the customer it may be necessary to again inspect or evaluate the product just before delivery to make sure that it has not degraded.

You need to have records that show that the product or service meets its established requirements. These records can vary from detailed measurement results listing numerical values for extremely large numbers of product characteristics, to just a simple stamp, signature, tag, or similar method showing that the product meets the requirements. The identity of the person or persons authorizing the release of the product must also be recorded. The needs of your product and requirements of your customer determine the amount of detail required in your operation.

You can determine how your inspection takes place. Individuals can inspect their own work, individuals in the next step of a process can check the output of the previous step, or you may have a dedicated individual release the product. You may use techniques such as process control charts or acceptance-sampling. The best methodology and final choice depends upon your product and your organization.

You should keep in mind, though, that it is difficult for people to evaluate their own output. The human mind will many times make the same mistake twice. If you have individuals evaluate and inspect their own work, you should consider the use of some mistake-proofing or auditing techniques.

The standard requires that you do not release the product or deliver the service until it has met its requirements, unless an authorized person (and, when applicable, the customer) approves the release.

Optional Documented Procedures

Determine what work instructions you might need to make sure your product is inspected and measured correctly.

Required Records

You must have records that show that the required acceptance criteria have been met. This does not mean that you need actual measurement records. What it does mean, though, is that there is a record that the product has been evaluated and meets requirements. The records must show the authority responsible for the release of the product. These records must be controlled.

 Techniques for Small and Medium Businesses

Most successful smaller businesses already have systems in place that enable them to deliver conforming product to their customers. If this is your situation, briefly describe your measurement and monitoring system in your quality manual.

Data analysis may indicate that you need to improve or revise your product measuring and monitoring system. If so, make the changes as necessary. This may or may not require a change in the information describing your system in your quality manual.

8.3 CONTROL OF NONCONFORMING PRODUCT

You need to make sure that nonconforming product is identified and controlled, to keep it from being unintentionally used or delivered, in one or more of the following ways:

- Take action to eliminate the detected nonconformity. Some possible methods of doing this include—

  - Reworking the product: a restaurant can put a steak back on the grill, a manufacturer can remachine a part.

  - Repairing the product: a fast food restaurant can add the tomatoes it forgot to put on a sandwich, a fabrication shop can re-weld and stress-relieve a weldment.

  - Scrapping the product: a fast food restaurant can discard a sandwich, a foundry can throw out a casting that is too small or has pinholes or inclusions.

  - Blending the product with conforming product: a technique used in process industries.

- Take action to prevent its original, intended use or application by downgrading the product to a use where it meets downgraded-product specifications. Using the material for a different product, for example, by making applesauce out of apples that can no longer be used for a Waldorf salad in a restaurant.

- Authorize its use, release, or acceptance under concession by a relevant authority and, where applicable, by the customer. This permits the "use as is" disposition of the nonconforming product. However, note that the standard requires this disposition to be approved by somebody that has the special authority to do so. Note, also, that a customer can require that they be included in the approval process.

The standard also requires that you reverify, reinspect, or retest the product that you have corrected, reworked, or repaired to make sure that it conforms to requirements.

The standard requires that you take action appropriate to the effects and/or potential effects of the nonconformity when it is discovered after delivery or use has started. This could mean doing nothing if a minor and noncritical dimension was out one-thousandth of an inch on the handle of a shovel, or it could mean recalling thousands of cars if a life-threatening error was discovered. A similar recall might be required if dangerous bacteria were discovered in some processed food.

Sometimes correcting nonconformances can be expensive. For example, an old processing technique was used without refinement on a new but similar product. The result was an in-process product that had a major defect in about 0.5 percent of the raw stock. The defect could be sorted out visually and by further processing. However, the further processing step was a high-speed operation and a product failure caused a short shutdown. All of the raw stock was inspected for the defect, and then acceptance samples inspected to verify the effectiveness of the 100 percent inspection. This was done until the process causing the problem was fine tuned so that it no longer produced the defect. The inspection consumed the efforts of 80 inspectors and three engineers for six weeks.

In another instance, the combination of an incorrect welding material and marginal stress relief furnace controls resulted in product that was at the high end of the hardness acceptance specification. A couple dozen extremely large and expensive weldments were produced under this condition. One of the weldments developed cracking, and in order to identify which ones to reprocess, the manufacturer sent a technician all over the world to test the product.

Required Documented Procedures

The standard requires that you have a documented procedure which defines the controls and related responsibilities and authorities for dealing with nonconforming product.

Required Records

The standard requires that you maintain records describing non-conformities found and any later actions taken. This record must include concessions obtained when applicable.

Techniques for Small and Medium Businesses

Again, the technique used in your business depends upon your product and your organization. Successful systems have used notes on production reports, diaries, or notes made by the appropriate personnel. The primary need is that this data be available for analysis of your quality system and its effectiveness. Unless you have complex needs, you may just want to describe what you do in your quality manual and then make sure you do it.

8.4 ANALYSIS OF DATA

Analysis of data is almost the most important element of ANSI/ISO/ASQ Q9001–2000. When your organization is committed to implementing ISO 9000, analysis of data provides feedback on the effectiveness and efficiency of your organization and your quality management system.

Your organization needs to:

- Determine the data that it needs

- Collect this data

- Analyze this data

Determining the data that you need is one of the more important steps. Data analysis for its own sake is often a useless exercise. In fact, it may have negative results because some may think that analysis is an ineffective process when positive results are not obtained. The members of your organization need to examine your processes and determine what data will give insight into these processes. Data collection methods can then be planned and implemented and analysis techniques determined.

Data analysis is necessary to demonstrate the suitability and effectiveness of your quality management system. Possibly even more important to you is the use of the data to show where continual improvement of your quality management system can be made.

The source of your data is from the measurement and monitoring that you performed, plus data from customers, customer surveys, and other sources, including those identified under subelement 8.2.1 "Customer satisfaction."

The analysis of data must provide information relating to:

- Customer satisfaction, as discussed under subelement 8.2.1 "Customer satisfaction"

- Conformance to product requirements, as discussed under subelement 7.2.1 "Determination of requirements related to the product"

- Characteristics and trends of processes and products, including opportunities for preventive action

- Suppliers

Data related to customer satisfaction is slightly different from data indicating whether or not the product conforms to requirements. Subelement 8.2.1 "Customer satisfaction" addresses customer perception of whether or not your organization has fulfilled its requirements. You may possibly provide a product that meets stated requirements, but the customer may still feel that its requirements have not been met. On the other hand, you may provide a technically nonconforming product that the customer is entirely satisfied with.

Data from product and process measurement and monitoring can be used for product and process analysis. You should, however, include data from customer feedback and any other relevant sources, both internal and external.

Supplier performance data, obtained through the processes of subelement 7.4.1 "Purchasing process," can be used to identify both excellent and poorly performing suppliers. Information and data gained from excellent suppliers can be used to either assist or remove poorly performing suppliers.

Optional Documented Procedures

You may want to have a procedure that describes your processes for the analysis of data and the actions to be taken as a result of the analyses.

Techniques for Small and Medium Businesses

In small and medium sized companies, collected data is provided directly to top management, who then conduct the analysis of the data as part of the management review.

Data planning, data gathering, and data analysis techniques for smaller organizations do not have to be as complex as they need to be for larger organizations. However, since this is an extremely important part of your quality management system, your management team needs to examine this element and plan their analyses processes.

8.5 IMPROVEMENT

8.5.1 Continual Improvement

You need to continually improve your quality management system, not just because the standard says you should but also because it means improved profitability. You use data analysis to find areas for improvement. You use corrective action when problems occur and then use preventive action to make sure that similar problems do not occur in other areas. Corrective action, preventive action, data analysis, and audit results are used in your management review. You need to examine your quality policy and objectives for modification and improvement, especially during your management review.

Techniques for Small and Medium Businesses

Use this element to briefly describe how your organization ties these various concepts together in your quality system to provide for and create continual improvement.

8.5.2 Corrective Action

You need a process to eliminate the cause of nonconformities. The process needs to include the reviewing of nonconformities and determining their root cause, which is the operation, quality system design, or similar problem that is the underlying source of product nonconformances. Examples of root causes may include:

- Inadequate or nonexistent procedures and documentation
- Noncompliance with procedures
- Inadequate process control
- Poor scheduling
- Lack of training
- Inadequate working conditions
- Inadequate human or material resources

Possible data sources for root cause analysis include:

- Inspection and test records
- Nonconformance records
- Observations during process monitoring
- Audit observations
- Field, service, or customer complaints
- Regulatory authority or customer observations
- Observations and reports by personnel
- Supplier problems
- Management review results
- Inherent process variability

Once the root causes are determined, your organization needs to decide if any actions should be taken, and what those actions should be, to make sure nonconformances do not recur.

Keep in mind that actions should be appropriate to the effects of the nonconformities encountered. Use the corrective action system to identify and correct situations that have the greatest impact on your quality management system effectiveness and overall product quality. The corrective action system is not intended to correct each and every nonconformance.

Once you have determined that action is necessary, implement and record the results of the action. Did the action correct the problem? Is additional action necessary? These and similar questions need to be asked and answered, and actions must be taken until the problem is corrected. Once the corrective action has been in place for a period of time, it should be reviewed again to make sure it is still effective.

Required Documented Procedures

The standard requires that you have a documented procedure that describes your corrective action system.

Required Records

The standard requires that you record the results of corrective actions taken.

 Techniques for Small and Medium Businesses

This is a problem area for many smaller businesses. Because many small and medium organizations have a shallow structure, corrections to problems are made on the fly. As a result they do not get documented. This can cause small organizations to "reinvent the wheel" by continually making the same correction without finding or identifying the existence of the root cause of the problem.

This is why it is important for your organization to develop and implement a simple corrective action

Continued

system following the requirements of the standard. In fact, the simpler you make it, the easier it will be for you to continue using it. Describe your basic corrective action system, and either refer to or include the procedure, in your quality manual.

Another improvement tool is the Plan, Do, Check (or Study), Act cycle developed by Shewhart and popularized by Deming. This cycle starts with establishing the objectives and the processes necessary to deliver results. The next step is to implement the processes. Then, study the processes against the objectives and take appropriate action. Continue with the cycle until the ultimate objective is reached.

8.5.3 Preventive Action

Many organizations use the same system for preventive and corrective action because they fail to see the difference between the concepts. However, because the concepts are different, the techniques are necessarily different. Corrective action is the solution of known problems, whereas preventive action is used to find potential causes of possible problems.

Your organization is required to identify preventive action to eliminate the cause of potential nonconformities. This does not mean that you have to identify every possible nonconformance that could occur. However, you need to identify the possible nonconformances for which you want to take preventive action.

Following are some techniques used to identify potential problems and their impacts:

• Aerospace, automotive, and other industries use failure mode effect and criticality analysis (FMECA), risk analysis, or similar techniques to identify products or parts of products whose failure can cause problems. The technique evaluates the probability that the failure will occur and the subsequent effect of the failure. As an example, the screw holding the license plate bracket on your car may result in a loose license plate if it breaks or falls out. However, if the nut holding the steering wheel onto the steering column fails, you may lose control of the vehicle.

- When nonconformances occur in one part of your quality system or one of your product lines, evaluate the corrective action taken to see if preventive action is needed in another area of your quality system or a similar product line.

- Process monitoring and measurement data may identify processes and product parameters that have increased probability of causing nonconformances.

- The management review program can be used to identify possible areas for preventive action through direct data analysis or by identifying weak areas through several inputs into the management review process.

Once you have determined that preventive action is necessary, you must implement the action, record its results, and review the preventive action later to make sure that it is still effective.

Required Documented Procedures

The standard requires that you have a documented procedure that describes your preventive action system.

Required Records

The standard requires that you record the results of preventive actions taken.

 Techniques for Small and Medium Businesses

Like corrective action, preventive action is a problem area for many small and medium businesses. Because many smaller business organizations have a shallow structure, corrections to problems are made on the fly. As a result they do not get documented. This can

Continued

cause small organizations to miss opportunities to identify preventive actions that can be applied to other product lines or areas of the quality system, and no efforts are made to use techniques such as FMECA.

This is why it is important for your organization to develop and implement a simple preventive action system. In fact, the simpler you make it, the easier it will be for you to continue using it. Consider using FMECA risk analysis or other techniques. Describe your basic preventive action system, and either refer to or include the procedure, in your quality manual.

Table 6.3 Suggested statistical techniques for an ANSI/ISO/ASQ Q9001–2000 quality management system.

ANSI/ISO/ASQ Q9001–2000 Clause and Subclause	Reasons for the Use of Statistical Techniques	Suggested Statistical Techniques
4 Quality management system		
4.1 General requirements	††	††
4.2 Documentation requirements		
4.2.1 General	††	††
4.2.2 Quality manual	††	††
4.2.3 Control of documents	Assess the extent to which documents are controlled.	Sampling.
4.2.4 Control of quality records	Assess the extent to which quality records are controlled.	Sampling.
5 Management responsibility		
5.1 Management commitment	Assess the extent to which the quality policy is implemented in your organization.	Sampling.
5.2 Customer focus	††	††

Continued

ANSI/ISO/ASQ Q9001–2000 Clause and Subclause	Reasons for the Use of Statistical Techniques	Suggested Statistical Techniques
5.3 Quality policy	Assess the extent to which the quality policy is implemented in your organization.	Sampling.
5.4 Planning		
5.4.1 Quality objectives	Assess the extent to which quality objectives are implemented in your organization.	Sampling.
5.4.2 Quality management system planning	††	††
5.5 Responsibility, authority and communication		
5.5.1 Responsibility and authority	††	††
5.5.2 Management representative	††	††
5.5.3 Internal communication	††	††
5.6 Management review		
5.6.1 General *5.6.2 Review input* *5.6.3 Review output*	Quantitatively measure your organization's performance against its quality objectives.	Descriptive statistics, sampling, SPC charts, trend analysis, easy graphical techniques.
6 Resource management		
6.1 Provision of resources	††	††
6.2 Human resources		
6.2.1 General *6.2.2 Competence, awareness and training*	Need to evaluate how well personnel are aware of the relevance and importance of their activities. Need to evaluate how well appropriate records of education, training, skills, and experience are maintained.	Sampling.
6.3 Infrastructure	**	**
6.4 Work environment	**	**

Continued

ANSI/ISO/ASQ Q9001–2000 Clause and Subclause	Reasons for the Use of Statistical Techniques	Suggested Statistical Techniques
7 Product realization		
7.1 Planning of product realization	See individual subelements.	See individual subelements.
7.2 Customer-related processes		
7.2.1 Determination of requirements related to the product	††	††
7.2.2 Review of requirements related to the product	Review product requirements to ensure that your organization has the capability to meet the requirements.	Process capability analysis, sampling, easy graphical techniques.
7.2.3 Customer communication	Seek customer feedback.	Sampling.
7.3 Design and development		
7.3.1 Design and development planning	Determine how well plans are updated.	Sampling.
7.3.2 Design and development inputs	Identify and review design input requirements for adequacy, and resolve differences.	Process capability analysis, sampling.
7.3.3 Design and development outputs	Determine if design outputs satisfy input requirements.	Descriptive statistics, process capability analysis, sampling, easy graphical techniques.
7.3.4 Design and development review	††	††
7.3.5 Design and development verification	Make sure that your design meets stated requirements.	Design of experiments, sampling.
7.3.6 Design and development validation	Make sure that the product conforms to defined user needs and/or requirements.	Sampling, descriptive statistics, easy graphical techniques.
7.3.7 Control of design and development changes	Evaluate how well the records of design and development review are maintained.	Sampling.

ANSI/ISO/ASQ Q9001–2000 Clause and Subclause	Reasons for the Use of Statistical Techniques	Suggested Statistical Techniques
7.4 Purchasing		
7.4.1 Purchasing process	Evaluate suppliers on the basis of their ability to meet requirements.	Descriptive statistics, process capability analysis, sampling, trend analysis, easy graphical techniques.
7.4.2 Purchasing information	††	††
7.4.3 Verification of purchased product	Inspect and test product as required to verify that the product conforms to specified requirements.	Descriptive statistics, sampling, easy graphical techniques.
7.5 Production and service provision		
7.5.1 Control of production and service provision	Make sure that your equipment is suitable. Monitor and control suitable process parameters and product characteristics. Maintain equipment to ensure continuing process capability. Specify inspection and test activities to verify that product requirements are met. Inspect and test product as required.	Descriptive statistics, process capability analysis, design of experiments, sampling, SPC charts, trend analysis, easy graphical techniques.
7.5.2 Validation of processes for production and service provision	Approve processes and equipment. Assure suitable maintenance of equipment to ensure continuing process capability.	Descriptive statistics, process capability analysis, sampling, SPC charts, trend analysis, easy graphical techniques.
7.5.3 Identification and traceability	Evaluate how well product identification and traceability is maintained.	Sampling.
7.5.4 Customer property	Evaluate how well records of unsuitable customer property are maintained.	Sampling.

Continued

ANSI/ISO/ASQ Q9001–2000 Clause and Subclause	Reasons for the Use of Statistical Techniques	Suggested Statistical Techniques
7.5.5 Preservation of product	Evaluate deterioration of product in stock to determine appropriate interval between assessments. Measure conformance of packaging, packing, and marking processes to specified require-ments. Evaluate adequacy of preservation and segregation of product under organization's control. Evaluate adequacy of protection of product quality after final inspection and test.	Descriptive statistics, process capability analysis, SPC charts, sampling, trend analysis, easy graphical techniques.
7.6 Control of monitoring and measuring devices	Evaluate capability of inspection, measure-ment, and test equipment. Develop the processes for calibration of inspection, measurement, and test equipment. Measure the validity of previous inspection and test results when equipment is found not to meet requirements.	Descriptive statistics, sampling, process capability analysis, SPC charts, trend analysis, easy graphical techniques.
8 Measurement, analysis and improvement		
8.1 General	††	††
8.2 Monitoring and measurement		
8.2.1 Customer satisfaction	††	††
8.2.2 Internal audit	Use sampling in planning and conducting internal audits. Summarize data from audits. Verify activities.	Descriptive statistics, sampling, easy graphical techniques.

ANSI/ISO/ASQ Q9001–2000 Clause and Subclause	Reasons for the Use of Statistical Techniques	Suggested Statistical Techniques
8.2.3 Monitoring and measurement of processes	Ensure the suitability of equipment. Monitor and control suitable process parameters and product characteristics. Evaluate maintenance of equipment to ensure continuing process capability. Specify inspection and test activities to verify that product requirements are met.	Descriptive statistics, process capability analysis, design of experiments, sampling, SPC charts, trend analysis, easy graphical techniques.
8.2.4 Monitoring and measurement of product	Inspect and test product as required. Verify that finished product conforms to specified requirements.	Descriptive statistics, process capability analysis, sampling, easy graphical techniques.
8.3 Control of nonconforming product	Analyze the cause of nonconforming product.	Descriptive statistics, design of experiments, process capability analysis, sampling, SPC charts, trend analysis.
8.4 Analysis of data	Collect and analyze data to demonstrate the suitability of the quality management system.	Descriptive statistics, design of experiments, process capability analysis, sampling, SPC charts, trend analysis, easy graphical techniques.
8.5 Improvement		
8.5.1 Continual improvement	Quantitative assessment of your organization's performance against its quality objectives.	Descriptive statistics, sampling, SPC charts, trend analysis, easy graphical techniques.
8.5.2 Corrective action	Assess effectiveness of your process for handling customer complaints and reports of nonconformances. Analyze the cause of nonconformances relating to product. Evaluate the effectiveness of corrective action.	Descriptive statistics, design of experiments, process capability analysis, sampling, SPC charts, trend analysis, easy graphical techniques.

Continued

ANSI/ISO/ASQ Q9001–2000 Clause and Subclause	Reasons for the Use of Statistical Techniques	Suggested Statistical Techniques
8.5.3 Preventive action	Summarize and analyze product or process data related to actual or potential nonconformities. Ensure the effectiveness of preventive action.	Descriptive statistics, design of experiments, process capability analysis, sampling, SPC charts, trend analysis, easy graphical techniques.

†† No use of statistical technique identified.
Source: Based on ISO/TR 10017 and ANSI/ISO/ASQ Q9001–2000.

Chapter 7

A Sample
Quality Manual

T his chapter is an example of a quality manual that can be
developed for a small company. Smokey and Ginger Writing Instruments Company (SnGWICO) is a fictitious organization. However, its manual and supporting documents show
that a viable ISO 9001 quality system can be established even for
very small companies and documented in a rather simple and
basic quality manual. This manual is based on experience gained
by the author in helping smaller companies develop and document their quality systems.

A LITTLE BACKGROUND

SnGWICO has been owned and operated by two quality profes-
sionals for about 17 years. The owners are certified and registered auditors. In addition, they hold several of the other
certifications offered by the quality profession. Both owners are
experienced woodworkers.

Exotic writing instruments are generally hand turned from
blanks made from rare and exotic woods, shed animal antlers,
and some colorful man-made materials. These blanks are bored
so that pen, ballpoint pen, ink pen, and palm computer styli
works can be inserted into the center. This technique allows the

production of unique eye-catching pens and pencils. The owners of these instruments are then proud of owning a beautiful and useful object of art. The works come in different styles and finishes. The quality challenge is finding a source of works that are both dimensionally consistent and reliable.

SnGWICO QUALITY MANUAL

4 Quality Management System

4.1 General Requirements

SnGWICO (pronounced S "n" G WICO) manufactures and services writing instruments made from exotic woods and similar materials. The exotic woods are obtained directly from nature or from wholesalers and other suppliers of exotic woods. The mechanisms of the writing instruments are purchased from wholesalers.

The primary processes of SnGWICO are administration, design and development, marketing and sales, purchasing, manufacturing and inspection, and servicing.

SnGWICO provides writing instruments using standard designs. The company also works directly with customers to provide product to the customer's specifications and designs. SnGWICO also repairs writing instruments made by SnGWICO and other manufacturers. The sequence of operations starts with marketing and/or sales determining customer requirements. The next step is design and/or development, when necessary, followed by manufacturing, inspection, packaging, and delivery. Support operations include development and administration of the quality system, planning, training, management review, resource management, monitoring and measuring, internal auditing, nonconforming product control, and continual improvement.

This quality manual covers the determination of the criteria and methods needed to:

- Ensure that the operation and control of the quality management processes are effective

- Assure the availability of resources and information necessary to support the operation of the processes

- Measure, monitor, and analyze these processes

- Implement actions necessary to achieve planned results and continuous improvement

No processes, other than possibly internal auditing, are outsourced. The external auditors, if used, must be either certified quality auditors or registered quality auditors.

4.2 Documentation Requirements

4.2.1 General

The quality policy of SnGWICO is to provide high-quality, handmade writing instruments using exotic woods and other exotic materials that are highly reliable and aesthetically pleasing. SnGWICO commits to complying with requirements and improving the effectiveness of the quality management system. The compliance to requirements is evaluated through internal audits and corrective actions. Improvement of the effectiveness of the quality management system is attained through corrective and preventive action. The quality objectives are to continually improve:

- The reliability of the products through improvements in design, manufacturing, and supplier improvement. This is measured through statistical analysis of reliability data obtained from sources such as supplier evaluations, manufacturing nonconformances, and customer complaints.

- The aesthetic appearance of the product, as measured by customer evaluations and comments obtained at the sale of the product.

The specific metrics and numeric goals are documented in the management review records.

4.2.2 Quality Manual

This quality manual describes the quality management system of SnGWICO. It covers the design, manufacturing, sales, service, and delivery of fine writing instruments provided by SnGWICO. SnGWICO does not use any processes where the resulting output cannot be verified by subsequent monitoring or measurement.

Therefore, subclause 7.5.2 "Validation of processes for production and service provision" is not addressed in this quality manual. SnGWICO customers do not require traceability; therefore traceability is not covered in this quality manual. This quality manual contains some of the simpler procedures. Additional documented procedures are included at the end of this manual. This quality manual describes the interactions among the processes of SnGWICO quality management system.

This manual describes the records that will be maintained.

4.2.3 Control of Documents

Quality procedure QMD 4.2.3 describes the procedure used by SnGWICO to control documents. This procedure describes the controls used to:

- Approve documents for adequacy prior to issue

- Review and update as necessary and reapprove documents

- Ensure that changes and the current revision status of documents are identified

- Ensure that relevant versions of applicable documents are available at points of use

- Ensure that documents remain legible and readily identifiable

- Ensure that documents of external origin are identified and their distribution controlled

- Prevent the unintended use of obsolete documents and apply suitable identification to them if they are retained for any purpose

4.2.4 Control of Records

Quality procedure QMD 4.2.4 describes the procedure used by SnGWICO to control records. The procedure describes how records are kept legible, readily identifiable, and retrievable. The procedure defines the controls used for the identification, storage, protection, retrieval, retention time, and disposition of records.

5 Management Responsibility

5.1 Management Commitment

All employees are trained in the importance of meeting customer requirements. At this point, there are no statutory or regulatory requirements. The quality policy and quality objectives are stated in this manual. Management reviews are conducted following 5.6. Resources are managed under 6.1.

5.2 Customer Focus

The owner and administrative partner ensure that customer requirements are determined and met with the aim of enhancing customer satisfaction through sections 7.2.1, 8.2.1, and other sections of this quality manual.

5.3 Quality Policy

The quality policy stated in this manual is appropriate to the purpose of the organization. It includes a commitment to comply with requirements and continually improve the effectiveness of a quality management system. It provides a framework for establishing and reviewing quality objectives. It is communicated within the organization. All employees have been trained in the quality policy and all new employees are trained at the time of hire. This training is documented in the personnel records. The understanding of the quality policy is evaluated through daily contact and evaluated and documented during internal audits.

5.4 Planning

5.4.1 Quality Objectives

The quality objectives of SnGWICO are documented in this quality manual.

5.4.2 Quality Management System Planning

The quality management system has been planned and is described in this quality manual. The integrity of the quality management system is maintained through training and implementation, as applicable, when changes are planned.

5.5 Responsibility, Authority, and Communication

5.5.1 Responsibility and Authority

The organization consists of the owner and an administrative partner. The partnership has been in place for 17 years and the responsibilities and authorities are well-known. If additional employees are hired, their responsibilities and authorities will be developed and communicated.

5.5.2 Management Representative

The management representative is the owner. The owner is responsible for ensuring that the processes needed for the quality management system are established, implemented, and maintained. The management representative reports to the administrative partner on the performance of the quality management system and any need for improvements. The management representative has and will continue to ensure the promotion of awareness of customer requirements throughout the organization.

5.5.3 Internal Communication

The owner and the administrative partner communicate verbally on a regular basis. Communication related to customer requirements, other key and customer communications, and supplier communications are documented. These documents are maintained in the appropriate files.

5.6 Management Review

5.6.1 General

The owner and administrative partner review the quality management system approximately every quarter to ensure its continuing suitability, adequacy, and effectiveness. The review assesses opportunities for improvement and the need for changes to the quality management system, including the quality policy and quality objectives. Minutes of the management review are maintained in the management review logbook.

5.6.2 Review Input

The management review includes information on results of audits, customer feedback, product performance, product conformity, status of preventive and corrective actions, follow-up actions from previous management reviews, changes that could affect the quality management system, and recommendations for improvement.

5.6.3 Review Output

The output from the management review includes any decisions and actions related to improvement of the effectiveness of the quality management system and its processes, improvement of the product related to customer requirements, and resource needs.

6 Resource Management

6.1 Provision of Resources

SnGWICO has implemented and maintained the quality management system and has continually improved its effectiveness. SnGWICO has and will continue to enhance customer satisfaction by meeting customer requirements.

6.2 Human Resources

6.2.1 General

Personnel performing work affecting product quality have been and will continue to be competent on the basis of appropriate education, training, skills, and experience.

6.2.2 Competence, Awareness, and Training

The owner and administrative partner must:

- Be able to effectively communicate verbally and through written word, as evidenced by a high school diploma or equivalent documentation

- Thoroughly understand ISO 9000 quality management systems, as evidenced through prior experience documented in their personnel records

Manufacturing and assembly personnel must be able to:

- Read and understand SnGWICO product and process documents, as evidenced through training and evaluations performed by the owner and documented in the manufacturing and assembly person's personnel records

- Produce wood-encased writing products using standard wood shop equipment through training and/or experience, as documented in their personnel record

Personnel are trained internally or externally through appropriate, specialized training facilities when training needs are identified. These training needs are usually limited to management training, safety training, and the use of woodworking equipment. All training is documented in employee personnel files listing the date(s) of the training and the qualification of the trainer. The qualification may be the signature of the trainer on a training completion document, from a recognized institution, in the subject matter of the training. The effectiveness of the training is evaluated by the owner through regular communication and evaluations conducted during audits and documented in the audit reports.

The owner and the administrative partner are aware of the relevance of their activities and how they contribute to the achievement of the quality objectives. This same awareness is communicated and evaluated with new personnel when they are hired. Personnel records hold the appropriate records of education, training, skills, and experience.

6.3 Infrastructure

SnGWICO has been in business for a long time, and current buildings, workspace, equipment, utilities, and support services have been and will continue to be adequate for the needs of the business.

6.4 Work Environment

SnGWICO's present work environment has been and will continue to be adequate to achieve conformity to product requirements.

7 Product Realization

7.1 Planning of Product Realization

The process for establishing quality objectives and requirements for the product is documented under 6.2.1.

The necessary processes, documents, and product-specific resources are set forth throughout these product realization sections of this quality manual.

The required verification, validation, monitoring, inspection, and test activities specific to SnGWICO writing instruments and the criteria for product acceptance are covered under sections 7 and 8 of this quality manual.

The records needed to provide evidence that the realization process and resulting product meet requirements are covered under sections 7 and 8 of this quality manual.

7.2 Customer-Related Processes

7.2.1 Determination of Requirements Related to the Product

Stock product is sold directly to the customer and it is assumed that product meets the customer requirements since it was purchased.

Repairs of writing instruments are performed at the point of sale. The customer requirements are determined and met to the highest degree possible.

For special orders, the customer orally communicates the product requirement giving the following information, as applicable:

- Quantity ordered

- Type of instrument (pencil, liquid-ink pen, ballpoint pen, special)

- Style of writing instrument (perfect, slimline, and so on)

- Types of wood or casing material

- Standard or special exterior shape (special exterior shapes are drawn to size on the sales document)

- Name and contact information of the customer

- Delivery requirements

The information is documented on the sales document that is initialed and dated by the SnGWICO representative. All writing instruments must write on applicable surfaces and leave the expected imprint.

There are no statutory or regulatory requirements for the product.

SnGWICO requires that the instrument must operate smoothly and be aesthetically pleasing.

7.2.2 Review of Requirements Related to the Product

Stock product and repair product reviews occur at the time of sale and delivery. The review is automatic and not documented.

The following process is followed for special orders. The owner or administrative partner reviews the sales document to verify that the product requirements are defined. Special exterior shape drawings are examined to verify that they can be produced using the type of material chosen. If there is a possible problem with obtaining the desired shape, an attainable shape is proposed. If this shape is not accepted by the customer, then the order is not accepted. Records of the review on special products are documented on the sales document by signature and date. When calls or other communications are received on special orders, the information is attached to the sales/production document and becomes a part of that document. If the new requirements cannot be met, the customer is contacted and the differences are resolved or the order is canceled.

7.2.3 Customer Communication

Product information and inquiries, and contracts or order handling, including amendments, are covered under 7.2.2.

Customer comments and complaints are documented on the sales document for later review. In addition, SnGWICO asks customers to enter comments in a customer comment book at the point of sale. SnGWICO also uses a customer comment and complaint logbook that is used to document verbal customer comments. Letters from customers are kept in the customer comments logbooks.

7.3 Design and Development

7.3.1 Design and Development Planning

Design and development of writing instruments provided by SnGWICO is accomplished by determining:

- The type of product (pencil, ink pen, and so on).

- The style of the product (stogie, slimline, and so on).

- The length and interior diameter(s) of the wood or other material casing, dictated by the style and type of product.

- The exterior shape and appearance, which can be stock or designed specifically for a customer. Stock shapes are detailed in a catalog.

- Special exterior shapes, developed by the customer and the SnGWICO owner.

The SnGWICO owner is responsible for all design steps on stock product. The SnGWICO owner and the customer manage their interface and are responsible for the design steps on special product. Planning does not have to be updated since design occurs in a short time frame.

7.3.2 Design and Development Inputs

The product requirements for SnGWICO writing instruments are documented under 7.2.1. Where applicable, information is derived from previous similar designs. These inputs are adequate; requirements are complete and are not ambiguous or in conflict with each other when new designs are being evaluated.

7.3.3 Design and Development Outputs

The design output consists of a manufacturing and assembly work instruction sheet developed for each style and type of writing instrument. The work instruction sheet gives the following information:

- Writing instrument mechanical parts to be used

- Mandrel size

- Barrel diameter(s) and length(s)

- Wood blank sizes

- Drill size(s)

- Bushing sizes and mandrel setup

- Assembly instructions

- Finishing instructions

- Acceptance criteria, including the characteristics of the product that are essential for its use

The scale drawing on the sales document is part of the design output for special writing instruments.

7.3.4 Design and Development Review

The design time for SnGWICO writing instruments is extremely short and usually accomplished in minutes or hours, at most. Therefore the design is approved when it is generated. The owner signs and dates the writing instrument work instructions to document the completion of the design review. For special writing instruments, both the customer and the owner or administrative partner sign the sales document. The SnGWICO signature indicates both the acceptance of the order as described above and the approval of the design.

7.3.5 Design and Development Verification

The SnGWICO product is a simple product. Therefore the design is considered to be verified when the review is approved.

7.3.6 Design and Development Validation

The writing instrument is tested to make sure that it performs its intended function and operates smoothly when it is completed and ready for delivery or placement in inventory. This test serves both as a design validation and acceptance test for the writing instrument.

7.3.7 Control of Design and Development Changes

Design and development changes are handled following 7.2.2.

7.4 Purchasing

7.4.1 Purchasing Process

SnGWICO uses two basic types of purchased materials. The mechanical parts of the writing instruments are purchased from wholesalers and standard vendor quality procedures can be used. The bodies of the writing instruments are made from natural product, usually organic. Only basic types of vendor quality assurance techniques, such as verification of the type of material ordered, rough dimensions, and board foot quantities, can be verified.

7.4.2 Purchasing Information

There are no requirements for qualification of personnel or quality management system requirements for product purchases.

Auditors are required to be certified quality auditors or registered auditors when internal audit services are purchased.

Writing instrument mechanisms are ordered using the wholesaler's catalog number that relates to a set of internal specifications for the wholesaler.

The exotic wood used for the bodies is either obtained direct from nature by the owner or purchased from a supplier. The owner usually selects purchased wood at the supplier's facility.

7.4.3 Verification of Purchased Product

Purchases of wood are verified when they are selected.

Shipments of writing instrument mechanisms are sample inspected using ANSI Z1.4 or ANSI Z1.9 upon receipt, if lot sizes are large enough. For smaller shipments, 100 percent inspection is used.

Shipments of mechanisms from an approved supplier are inspected only for quantity and shipping damage. The determination of the techniques to be used is based upon the characteristic of the product and prior supplier history. Records of the inspection are maintained on or with the shipping documents and invoices. The record is signed by the owner as verification of inspection and its results.

7.5 Production and Service Provision

7.5.1 Control of Production and Service Provision

The information describing the characteristics of the object is on the manufacturing and assembly work instructions.

Standard, proven, brand-name woodworking equipment is used.

Micrometers, scales, and calipers are used to measure the product and monitor the operations.

Monitoring and measuring are described under 8.2.3 and 8.2.4.

Release, delivery, and post-delivery activities are performed following applicable portions of section 8.

7.5.3 Identification and Traceability

Traceability is not a requirement for SnGWICO products.

The product is identified by the accompanying work instructions. Special product is further identified by the accompanying sales document. Inventories of wood are identified by type of wood when it is not obvious by observation. Writing instrument mechanical parts are identified on the package. Labels on parts bins identify spare parts. In addition, most spare parts are identifiable by observation.

7.5.4 Customer Property

Writing instrument repair is performed while the customer waits. SnGWICO tries to protect and safeguard the customer's product properly when it is being repaired. If the owner feels that the repair cannot be safely made, the repair is refused.

7.5.5 Preservation of Product

Completed writing instruments are placed in protective sleeves or boxes. Writing instruments are shipped, when necessary, in padded mail envelopes.

7.6 Control of Monitoring and Measuring Devices

Scales and calipers are used for rough dimensional measurement. Their condition is monitored and they are replaced when deemed necessary.

A zero- to one-inch micrometer is used for precision measurement of barrels, bushings, and mandrels. The micrometer is calibrated annually or when it is thought that it might be damaged. A qualified calibration laboratory performs the calibration. The scales, calipers, and micrometer are checked against measurement standards monthly. The measurement standards are calibrated or replaced every 10 years.

These instruments are used for receiving and in-process inspection. When equipment is found not to conform to requirements, it will only affect the assembly and function test of the product. Therefore, recall of product would not be necessary.

Computer software is not used in the measuring and monitoring of specified requirements.

8 Measurement, Analysis, and Improvement

8.1 General

Measurement, monitoring, analysis, and improvement to demonstrate the conformity of the product is discussed under 8.2.4 and other portions of section 8.

Measurement, monitoring, analysis, and improvement to insure the conformity of the quality management system and to continually improve its effectiveness are discussed throughout section 8.

8.2 Monitoring and Measurement

8.2.1 Customer Satisfaction

SnGWICO uses a customer comment logbook for verbal comments received, a customer comment book which customers are asked to use at the time of purchase, and comments noted on the sales document by the customer at the time of purchase. These tools are used as measurements of the performance of SnGWICO quality management system.

8.2.2 Internal Audit

SnGWICO conducts internal audits on a quarterly basis to determine whether the quality management system conforms to

SnGWICO requirements, this quality manual, and related procedures, and the requirements of ISO 9001. The audit is also used to determine if the quality management system is effectively implemented and maintained.

The entire management system is audited at the time of audit. A checklist has been developed following ISO 9001 and this quality manual. Standard quality auditing methods following ISO audit standards are used. The administrative partner audits the work of the owner, and vice versa. Both are certified quality auditors.

Quality procedure 8.2.2 "Internal audit" contains the responsibilities and requirements for planning and conducting the audits, reporting the results, and maintaining records. The procedure also describes the corrective and preventive action and the correction processes used in response to the audits and describes how follow-up, verification, and related reporting are accomplished.

8.2.3 Monitoring and Measurement of Processes

Customer comments, nonconformance reports, and vendor evaluations are used to identify SnGWICO processes that need to be monitored and/or measured. Appropriate statistical tools, such as process capability analysis, sampling, descriptive statistics, statistical process control charts, and trend analysis, are used as applicable.

8.2.4 Monitoring and Measurement of Product

Writing instrument mechanisms packages are inspected dimensionally against the suppliers' specifications. The mechanisms are also tested for smooth operation.

Bushings, outside calipers, and scales are used to measure the writing instrument barrels as they are being produced. After the writing instruments have been assembled, they are tested for smooth operation and visual appearance. The assembler inserts an "accepted by inspector name" in the sleeve or box to authorize the release of the product. For special orders, the assembler also signs the sales document with an "OK," the assembler's initials, and date.

Neither product release or service delivery proceeds until the product meets specifications.

8.3 Control of Nonconforming Product

SnGWICO makes sure that product that does not conform to product requirements is identified and controlled to prevent its unintended use or delivery. The controls and related responsibilities and authorities for dealing with nonconforming product are defined in quality procedure 8.3.

Nonconforming mechanisms and disposition are documented on the receiving papers. Nonconforming writing instruments and disposition are documented on the work instructions for stock runs and on the sales document for special orders or repairs. Nonconforming wood is scrapped. Nonconforming writing mechanisms are kept separate and are returned to the vendor. Nonconforming spare parts are discarded. Nonconforming wood casings are broken off the barrels. The barrels are returned to stock and the wood is discarded.

Nonconforming assemblies that do not operate smoothly can be repaired. The repair is documented on the work instructions or the sales document. The writing instrument is then retested and inspected, and the release noted on the work instructions or sales document.

Product is tested again for functionality and inspected for appearance immediately prior to delivery to the customer. Therefore, nonconforming product cannot occur after delivery or use has started. However, if the customer experiences problems after receipt, SnGWICO repairs the product at no charge if it is returned within six months.

8.4 Analysis of Data

SnGWICO collects and analyzes customer comments, supplier evaluation results, nonconforming product reports, audit results, and corrective and preventive actions to demonstrate the suitability and effectiveness of its quality management system, and to determine where continual improvement of the effectiveness of the quality management system can be made. This analysis is performed at least quarterly prior to management review. It may be done more frequently if the owner decides that it is necessary, or appropriate beneficial statistical techniques are used.

8.5 Improvement

8.5.1 Continual Improvement

SnGWICO continually improves the effectiveness of the quality management system through the use of management reviews that include audit results, analysis of data, and corrective and preventive action. The management review is used to examine the quality policy and quality objectives.

8.5.2 Corrective Action

SnGWICO takes action to eliminate the cause of nonconformities in order to prevent recurrence. Corrective actions are appropriate to the effects of the nonconformities encountered. The owner determines when actions are necessary.

Quality procedure 8.5.2 describes the SnGWICO corrective action procedure. Corrective actions are documented in the corrective action logbook. The procedure defines the requirements for reviewing nonconformities, determining the causes of nonconformity, evaluating the need for action to ensure that nonconformities do not recur, determining and implementing action needed, and reviewing the action taken.

8.5.3 Preventive Action

SnGWICO determines action to eliminate the cause of potential nonconformities in order to prevent their occurrence. Preventive actions are appropriate to the effects of potential problems as determined by the owner. Quality procedure 8.5.3 describes SnGWICO's preventive action process. The procedure defines the requirements for determining potential nonconformities and their causes, evaluating the need for action to prevent occurrence of nonconformities, determining and implementing action needed, and reviewing preventive action taken. Preventive action records are maintained in the preventive action logbook.

SnGWICO
Quality procedure QMD 4.2.4 Control of records
December 22, 2000

Approved by Charles Hebert, Owner
Supersedes: New

[1]1.1 Records are handled following the processes described in the applicable sections of the quality manual. These processes document how the records demonstrate the achievement of the required quality. Pertinent supplier records, as explained in the procedures, are considered records to be maintained by SnGWICO.

The following list addresses the document management aspects of the various SnGWICO records:

- Management review logbook

- Education, training, skills, and experience

- Receiving paperwork, results of supplier evaluations, actions arising from supplier evaluations, and supplier communications

- Sales records, customer communications, and completed work instructions

- Customer comment logs

- Stock product work instructions

- Results of calibration and verification of measuring equipment

- Internal audit results

- Corrective action logbooks

- Preventive action logbooks

Italicized underlines indicate changes.

---

[1]This procedure is an example that is applicable only to the fictitious organization SnGWICO. It should not be copied and applied to any other organization.

SnGWICO
Quality procedure QMD 4.2.4 Control of records
December 22, 2000

Approved by Charles Hebert, Owner
Supersedes: New

1.2 Record management elements are listed in Table QMD.1. The primary record management characteristics are shown for SnGWICO documents and records in Table QMD.2.

1.3 SnGWICO prevents degradation of records by storing them in normal record filing or storage equipment (for example, file cabinets, file storage boxes, electronic archives). The adequacy of the environment is determined by the records' usable condition at the end of the minimum storage period.

1.4 Records shall be considered retrievable if they can be obtained in a reasonable period of time. Recent records are generally retrievable within hours. Older records may take longer to retrieve (for example, days), especially if they have been archived off site.

Table QMD.1	Record management elements.
Content	What information or record is in the record or file. If it is a compilation of subrecords, list the titles of the subrecords.
Identification	Title and unique identifier. Title should be meaningful and reflect purpose of the record. Numeric and alphanumeric codes can be used. Identifiers can include revision number and date.
Indexing	Identifies the information in the record and possibly the location. A record may have more than one identifier.
Access	How access is attained and who is allowed.
Retention	Retention time.
Maintenance	How are records maintained in useable condition for retention time?
Disposition	Record disposal.

Italicized underlines indicate changes.

SnGWICO
Quality procedure QMD 4.2.4 Control of records
December 22, 2000

Approved by Charles Hebert, Owner
Supersedes: New

Table QMD.2 Primary record management characteristics.

Content	Management review, customer comment logs, corrective and preventive action logs	Employee records
Identification	"Title" (e.g., Management Review) Log	Employee name
Indexing	Date	Alphabetical by employee
Access	All	Owner, administrative partner, employee
Retention	2 years	7 years
Maintenance	In owner's bookshelf in air-conditioned office	File cabinet in air-conditioned office
Disposition	Incinerate	Shred or incinerate

Content	Supplier records	Sales records
Identification	Supplier	Customer
Indexing	Alphabetical by supplier by date	Alphabetical by customer by date
Access	All	All
Retention	2 years	5 years
Maintenance	File cabinet in air-conditioned office	File cabinet in air-conditioned office
Disposition	Shred or incinerate	Shred or incinerate

Continued

Italicized underlines indicate changes.

SnGWICO
Quality procedure QMD 4.2.4 Control of records
December 22, 2000

Approved by Charles Hebert, Owner
Supersedes: New

Content	Stock product work instructions	Calibration records
Identification	Type and style	Instrument type and serial number
Indexing	By style by type	By instrument by serial number
Access	All	All
Retention	20 years	2 years
Maintenance	File cabinet in air-conditioned office	File cabinet in air-conditioned office
Disposition	Shred or incinerate	Shred or incinerate

Content	Audit records	
Identification	Audit record	
Indexing	Audit date	
Access	All	
Retention	3 years	
Maintenance	File cabinet in air-conditioned office	
Disposition	Shred or incinerate	

Italicized underlines indicate changes.

Bibliography

ANSI/ISO/ASQ Q9000–2000: *Quality management systems— Fundamentals and vocabulary.*

ANSI/ISO/ASQ Q9001–2000:*Quality management systems— Requirements.*

ANSI/ISO/ASQ Q9004–2000: *Quality management systems— Guidelines for performance improvements.*

Burr, John T. *SPC Tools for Everyone.* Milwaukee, WI: ASQC Quality Press, 1993.

Galloway, Dianne. *Mapping Work Processes.* Milwaukee, WI: ASQC Quality Press, 1994.

ISO 10005:1995, *Quality management—Guidelines for quality plans.*

ISO 10011-1:1990, *Guidelines for auditing systems— Part 1: Auditing*[1]

ISO 10011-2:1991, *Guidelines for auditing quality systems— Part 2: Qualification criteria for quality systems auditors*[1]

ISO 10011-3:1991, *Guidelines for auditing quality systems— Part 3: Management of audit programmes*[1]

---

[1]To be revised as ISO 19001, Guidelines on quality and/or environmental management systems auditing.

ISO 10012-1:1992, *Quality assurance requirements for measuring equipment—Part 1: Metrological confirmation system for measuring equipment.*

ISO 10012-2:1997, *Quality assurance for measuring equipment—Part 2: Guidelines for control of measurement processes.*

ISO/TR 10017:1999, *Guidance on statistical techniques for ISO 9001:1994.*

ISO 11462-1:2000, *Guidelines for the implementation of statistical process control (SPC)—Part 1: Elements of SPC*

ISO Survey '99—an analytical tool to assess the costs, benefits and savings of ISO 9000 Registration. A special report prepared by Quality Systems Update and Plexus Corporation

Quality Management Principles Brochure[2]

Reference Web sites:
1. http://www.iso.ch
2. http://www.bsi.org.k/iso-tc176-sc2

---

[2]Available from Web site: http://www.iso.ch

Index

product requirements, 66–69
purchasing, 83–87

Q

quality management principles, 12–13
quality management system, clause 4,
    23–39
  documentation requirements,
    27–39
    control of documents, 32–35
    control of records, 35–39
    general, 27–30
    quality manual, 30–32
  general requirements, 23–26
quality management system
  planning, 47–49
quality manual, 30–32
quality objectives, 47–49
quality plans, 65
quality policy, 45–46
quality system, 16

R

records, control of, 35–39
records, required, *31*
required
  documented procedures, 27
  documents, 29
  records, *31*
resource management, clause 6,
  57–62
  human resources, 58–60
    competence, awareness, and
      training, 58–60
    general, 58
  infrastructure, 60–61
  provision of resources, 57
  work environment, 61–62
resources, provision of, 57
responsibility and authority, 50

review
  design and development, 76–78
  management, 52–55
root cause, 116

S

sample quality manual, 127–148
scope, clause 1, 9–12
  application, 9–12
  general, 9
statistical techniques, 99–101,
  101–102, 120–126
supplier relationships, mutually
  beneficial, as quality
  management principle, 13
supply chain, 15

T

terms and definitions, clause 3,
  14–15, 15–16
top management, responsibilities of,
  41–55
traceability, and identification, 91–92
training, of employees, 58–60

V

validation studies of ANSI/ISO/ASQ
  Q9000–2000 draft standards, 4
validation
  design and development, 79–80
  of processes, 90–91
verification
  design and development, 78–79
  of purchased product, 85–87

W

work environment, 61–62